CLASSROOM MANAGEMENT

CLASSROOM MANAGEMENT

A Guide for the School Consultant

By

JACK TANAKA

*Institute for Juvenile Research
Department of Mental Health
State of Illinois
and
Neuropsychiatric Institute
University of Illinois
Chicago, Illinois*

CHARLES C THOMAS • PUBLISHER
Springfield • Illinois • U.S.A.

Published and Distributed Throughout the World by
CHARLES C THOMAS ● PUBLISHER
Bannerstone House
301-327 East Lawrence Avenue, Springfield, Illinois, U.S.A.

This book is protected by copyright. No part of it may be reproduced in any manner without written permission from the publisher.

© *1979, by* CHARLES C THOMAS ● PUBLISHER
ISBN 0-398-03858-9
Library of Congress Catalog Card Number: 78-9946

With THOMAS BOOKS *careful attention is given to all details of manufacturing and design. It is the Publisher's desire to present books that are satisfactory as to their physical qualities and artistic possibilities and appropriate for their particular use.* THOMAS BOOKS *will be true to those laws of quality that assure a good name and good will.*

Printed in the United States of America
V-R-1

Library of Congress Cataloging in Publication Data
Tanaka, Jack, 1943-
   Classroom management.

   Includes index.
   1. Classroom management. 2. Behavior modification.
3. Elementary school teachers--In-service training.
I. Title.
LB3013.T35   372.1′1′02   78-9946
ISBN 0-398-03858-9

INTRODUCTION

EDUCATORS, school psychologists, social workers, and numerous other professionals and paraprofessionals from community social service agencies working cooperatively with elementary school systems are well aware of teacher concerns about the behavioral problems of students. These problems — hyperactivity, indifference, lack of motivation, defiance — often frustrate the teacher whose efforts to remedy them are unsuccessful. Unable to cope or to utilize his or her teaching skills to foster student academic achievement, the teacher may become discouraged and disillusioned about teaching. In despair, the teacher may look for assistance in coping with problem student behaviors. Consider, for example, the following story, which is too often true.

Three or four kids were dancing in the coat room. Another kid, Steven, was crawling along the back of the classroom, sneaking up on Tina who was sleeping at her desk. Steven's sly grin was a signal that he was up to no good. Steven and Tina remained unnoticed by the teacher who, with a strained expression on her face, was trying to restrain Robert from crowning another kid with the window pole. The window pole swung wildly in the air as the teacher and student struggled for control of it. Willy, the target of the crowning, huddled under the teacher's desk, peering out occasionally to make obscene hand and facial gestures to egg Robert on. Students were screaming and running on top of the desks. Milk cartons and erasers flew through the air.

Soon the disruption overflowed into the hall. Several students were chasing each other and teasing the hall monitor. Others were peering into neighboring classrooms, waving at their friends. The teacher, holding the window pole, angrily yelled for them to "get back in here at once" but to little avail. Several other teachers came into the hall. They managed to corral two of the students and dragged them into the principal's office.

It was another bad day for the teacher of the low level fourth grade class, the class commonly referred to as the "zoo." The disruption was worse than on most of the previous days but even during the "best days" the teacher spent most of her time policing the classroom and attending to disruptions. This was the teacher's second year of teaching. The enthusiasm with which she began her teaching career was gone. Frustration and anger had replaced it. She now dreaded hearing the nine o'clock school bell that began her six hours of torment.

Not only was she becoming disillusioned with her education, the school system, the principal, parents, and students, she also had begun to question her teaching abilities. She had done well in college, but much of what she had learned did not seem to work. "If only the students would sit down, behave themselves, and listen, I could teach them something." She had had several discussions with her principal but felt more reprimanded than helped. She wrote notes home to the parents but most did not respond. She sought consultation from the school social worker and then the school psychologists. They, however, were able to meet with her only two or three times and were not of much help. Meanwhile, the principal continued to express concern for the poor conduct and achievement of her students and the school engineer complained about the litter and disarray of her classroom at the end of each day. The students were becoming bolder and more defiant. Out of desperation, but with little hope, the teacher reluctantly consented to meet with another consultant.

This manual has been written for those consultants, either within the school system or from a community agency, who may be called upon to assist a grammar school teacher with a problem such as this. A number of subjects are presented that should be considered by the consultant as he or she attempts to apply behavioral principles in a teacher consultation program.

Emphasis is placed on a problem solving model of consultation that will encourage the teacher to develop the classroom management skills involved in the remediation of problematic student behaviors and the establishment of desirable student behaviors. This manual also provides both a conceptual and procedural orientation for the consultant as he or she proceeds in consultation. The development of a classroom management program involving the use of a point system is used to illustrate the use of behavioral procedures in managing student behaviors. The subjects of the manual are presented according to the writer's perception of the order in which such subjects would ideally be addressed in the course of consultation. Since, however, the manner and order in which these subjects are addressed in an actual consultation frequently vary with opportunity and necessity, this manual should not be viewed as an absolute formula for every consultation involving classroom management problems. Rather, the manual should be examined in its entirety before considering its use as a reference for an actual consultation.

The manual is organized into three parts. Part I, "Preparation for Consultation," concerns issues that should be considered by the consultant as he or she plans to provide consultation. Emphasized here is the necessity for the consultant to establish a conceptual frame of reference before providing consultation. The various chapters of Part I present criteria for defining the role of the consultant, issues that should be clarified during the initial meetings and negotiations with the school principal and teachers, and the basic behavioral principles that should be mutually understood by the consultant and teacher. Part II, "Problem Solving," introduces a series of tasks that are to be accomplished by the consultant and teacher during the consultation. Each chapter in Part II presents a separate task as well as considerations and procedures involved in accomplishing that task. The completion, in order, of these problem solving tasks establishes the basis for the development of procedures to manage student behaviors in the classroom and provides the teacher with an understanding of the problem solving process. An example of a classroom management program, outlining procedures and forms, concludes Part II. Part III, "Consultation Experiences," presents some of the situations, personalities, perceptions, and concerns that may be encountered while providing consultation. A hypothetical consultant's log is used as a format for reviewing some of the affective components involved in a consultation. Actual teacher comments about their consultation experiences are presented. These comments provide a perspective of teacher perceptions of various aspects of the consultation. A glossary of terms and a selected reading list conclude the manual.

ACKNOWLEDGMENTS

I GRATEFULLY acknowledge the people who assisted in the preparation of this manual. Many thanks are owed to Dr. John L. Dodds, friend and English professor, for editing this manual and for the days spent in helping to express much of its content into coherent written words; Sharon Tanaka, my dearly loved wife and colleague, and Dr. Wesley Lamb, friend and colleague, for their comments, suggestions, and lasting support; and Marguerite Wilks and Joycelyn Thomas for typing this manual and correcting mistakes. Thanks also to the many others with whom I have worked and consulted and learned from — though I cannot adequately express my appreciation.

J.T.

CONTENTS

Page

Introduction v
Acknowledgments ix

Part I
PREPARATION FOR CONSULTATION

Chapter

1. THE ROLE OF THE CONSULTANT 5
2. NEGOTIATIONS 14
3. BEHAVIORAL PRINCIPLES 24

Part II
PROBLEM SOLVING

4. SPECIFYING PROBLEM STUDENT BEHAVIORS 39
5. ASSESSING PROBLEM STUDENT BEHAVIORS 49
6. MEASURING BEHAVIORS 56
7. SPECIFYING DESIRABLE STUDENT BEHAVIORS 65
8. IDENTIFYING POSITIVE REINFORCERS 71
9. SPECIFYING CONTINGENT RELATIONSHIPS 79
10. DEVELOPING POSITIVE TEACHER-STUDENT INTERACTIONS ... 88
11. A CLASSROOM MANAGEMENT PROGRAM 95

Part III
CONSULTATION EXPERIENCES

12. A CONSULTANT'S LOG 141
13. TEACHER COMMENTS AND EVALUATIONS 171

Appendix

    1. Glossary 191
    2. Selected Readings 194

Index 195

CLASSROOM MANAGEMENT

Part I
Preparation for Consultation

School consultation may include a broad range of activities and involve numerous school personnel addressing a variety of problem areas. Within this broad context, it is very difficult for the consultant to function effectively. The consultant must define his or her role as a consultant, identify the areas of agreement that should be negotiated with the teacher and principal, and acquire an understanding of the behavioral principles upon which the development of classroom management procedures are based. These topics are addressed in this order in the chapters of Part I.

Chapter 1

THE ROLE OF THE CONSULTANT

THOSE who act as consultants to teachers may occasionally find themselves in situations where they are not sure how to proceed. As consultants, they may feel obligated to respond to requests for assistance even when these requests involve knowledge or skills that are not within their area of expertise or responsibility. Frequently the first question asked by the consultant is "How can I be of help?" This suggests that the consultant is willing and able to respond to whatever the need of the teacher happens to be. It should, however, be understood that this is not always the case. Before this question is posed, the services that can be effectively provided by the consultant should be clearly understood. The first step in providing school consultation is to clarify the role of the consultant. In doing this, the following topics should be addressed: restrictions on the consultant, the tasks and goals to be accomplished, and the responsibilities of the consultant.

Restrictions on the Consultant

The desire to help a teacher, although admirable, is not sufficient. There are numerous restrictions that affect the consultant's ability to help, regardless of whether the consultant is from an outside agency or is part of the school system. Restrictions on the consultant include the amount of time available for each consultation, an individual's knowledge and skills, responsibilities to the employing agency, the resources available to support the consultation, and the degree of cooperation among the consultant, teacher, and principal. It is the consultant's responsibility to identify and account for these restrictions as he or she plans to provide consultation. The consultant must determine what help can be offered and how it can best be provided under the restrictions that exist.

The Targets of the Consultation

Much of the formal education of teachers focuses on the development of skills that are directed to the academic achievement of students. Their studies include curricula design, lesson planning, and the use of a variety of instructional materials and aids. Many teacher education curricula also include an educational psychology course that surveys the principles and procedures for establishing desirable student behaviors in the classroom. It is not until they are in actual classrooms, however, that teachers gain the practical experiences and skills necessary to manage student behaviors successfully. Many teachers, unfortunately, either do not profit from these experiences or fail to acquire the skills necessary to use the behavioral principles they learned in college. Some are simply overwhelmed by the severity of disruptive behaviors occurring in their classrooms. Others find themselves in the role of disciplinarians who must spend large portions of their classroom day patrolling the class, trying to keep their students from getting out of hand. Still others seem to develop the skills necessary to maintain productive student behaviors within a harmonious classroom atmosphere.

From the perspective of this manual, the purpose of school consultation is to assist the teacher in developing these kinds of skills, skills that will not only enhance the teacher's ability to manage student behaviors but will also indirectly foster greater academic and social growth in the students. To fulfill this purpose, the consultant must help the teacher develop those problem solving skills, both conceptual and procedural, that are involved in the management of student behaviors. Thus, the target of the consultation is not solely the remediation of problem student behaviors, but also the development of the teacher's ability to do so.

The Tasks and Goals of the Consultation

As part of the preparation to provide consultation, the consultant should also clearly delineate the tasks to be accomplished. From the perspective of this manual, these tasks can be divided into two categories. The first category of tasks concerns the gathering of information necessary to correct problem student behaviors and to develop the teacher's conceptual understanding of the problem solving process. These tasks include the following:

the specification of problem student behaviors
the assessment of problem student behaviors
the measurement of behaviors
the specification of desirable student behaviors
the identification of reinforcers
the specification of contingent relationships
the development of positive teacher-student interactions

The second category of tasks involves the application of behavioral principles by the teacher within the classroom setting. These tasks include the following:

the development of appropriate classroom management procedures
assisting the teacher in the remediation of problem student behaviors
providing practical advice and experiences so that the teacher can further apply and develop problem solving skills

The goals of these tasks are to establish desirable student behaviors, to establish the teacher as a positive reinforcer, to develop student self-management skills, and to maintain desirable student behaviors in a natural classroom environment.

Responsibilities of the Consultant

The consultant must always remember that assisting the teacher to develop problem solving skills does not mean assuming primary responsibility for the behaviors of the students. Though the consultant and students may interact directly as part of an assessment or for demonstration purposes, the interaction should not primarily be between the consultant and the students. If the interaction remains primarily between the consultant and the students, this program might be viewed as direct services to students rather than consultation with teachers. It should be mutually understood by the teacher and consultant that the teacher maintains responsibility for the students and the subsequent changes in their behaviors. The consultant *assists* the teacher.

Similarly, the teacher should also understand that the problems addressed during the consultation are those resulting from student behaviors in the classroom. Addressing the personal problems of a teacher that result from marital, family, or home difficulties should not be viewed as part of the role of the school consultant. To respond to personal problems is to provide therapy to the teacher. Both consultation and therapy may be valuable services to offer a school, but since the tasks and goals of each are different, it is important to maintain a distinction between them. The school consultant cannot effectively play two roles at one time. In this manual, the school consultant addresses the problems the teacher encounters as a teacher.

To develop a teacher's classroom management skills, behavioral principles should be utilized. Just as a teacher should apply behavioral principles to facilitate desirable changes in student behaviors, the consultant should apply these principles to facilitate the development of the teacher's skills. The application of behavioral principles by the consultant is essential both to the development of the teacher's skills and the maintenance of the teacher's cooperation. The consultant should provide appropriate cues and reinforcers for the development of the teacher's problem solving skills. The consultant also should emphasize the teacher's strengths by noting whenever possible what the teacher does well. Modeling, role-playing, and rehearsals can facilitate this process. Other means to assist the teacher in learning each of the problem solving tasks include the use of teacher records, outlines, and checklists — each of these will be covered in this manual.

The consultant should also identify possible reinforcers for the teacher's efforts. These might include recognition and encouragement by the school principal for the extra work involved in the consultation, time off from school responsibilities to compensate for after-school work done by the teacher, or even credit towards tenure or promotion. It should be understood, however, that the primary source of reinforcement for the teacher's efforts to develop problem solving skills should be the desirable changes in student behaviors.

Once the role of the consultant has been clarified and the tasks and goals of the consultation identified, he or she has established a basis for negotiations for consultation services. Before negotiations begin it is often helpful to provide the teacher and principal with a written proposal defining the consultant's role. This proposal should outline the general goals, format, and topics to be covered during the consultation. An example of a general consultation proposal follows. The proposal may be accompanied by a memo if the consultant is employed by the school or by a cover letter if the consultant is from an outside agency.

Sample Letter to a School

Dear (principal or other school official):

   The (school department or community agency name) is offering to teachers consultation services for the application of behavioral principles in the classroom management of student behaviors. This service is offered in response to the growing emphasis on the school's responsibility to provide remedial services for problem students. The consultation focusses on the development of teacher skills to reduce disruptive student behaviors and establish desirable behaviors compatible with student academic achievement. The consultation involves teacher training in student management procedures, the development of a classroom management program, and assistance to the teacher in implementing this program in his or her classroom. A general description of the consultation, which further outlines the topics, format, and activities, is attached. Please discuss this service with your teaching staff, especially those responsible for social adjustment classrooms or ones who have severe student behavioral problems in their classes. I will contact you within two weeks to discuss the consultation services and to arrange meetings with teachers who may be interested in participating. Please do not hesitate to call me if you desire further information.

                              Sincerely,

                              (the consultant)

Sample Proposal

TEACHER CONSULTATION
IN
THE CLASSROOM MANAGEMENT OF STUDENT BEHAVIORS

Teacher consultation will include readings, videotapes, films, and discussions on the application of behavioral principles involved in the management of student behaviors in the classroom. Participating teachers will be assisted in the development and implementation of a classroom management program for their classrooms. The classroom management program will consist of a point system and structured teacher interaction with the students in the class. The primary emphasis in training will be on the application of behavioral principles by the participating teachers in their classrooms. The consultation is thus a cooperative effort with the teachers and the consultant assuming various responsibilities for providing effective services to the children.

Teacher Responsibilities

Weekly one to two hour meetings will be scheduled with the participating teachers. These meetings will be held at the school during times when the teacher is available (library periods, gym, etc.) or when a teacher aide substitutes in the classroom. During these meetings, problem behaviors occurring in the teacher's classroom and behavioral techniques involved in the classroom management program will be discussed. Readings will be reviewed, films and videotapes will be viewed, and information on classroom observations will be given. The teachers will be responsible for preparing for these meetings.

The teacher will be primarily responsible for the implementation of the point system, related record keeping, and for consistently following the guidelines for teacher-student interactions. The cooperation, interest, and flexibility of the teacher in adopting new classroom procedures are essential criteria for participating.

The program is meant to deal with the behaviors of the students in the classroom. This assumes that the lesson plans and instructional material are appropriate for the students. The preparation of lessons and instructional material remains the primary responsibility of the classroom teachers.

Consultant Responsibilities

The consultant will make periodic classroom observations. Periodic videotapes of the class may also be made. The observations and videotapes will be used to provide information to the teacher on how well the program is being implemented. These will be reviewed during the weekly meetings, as will classroom records kept by the teacher.

The consultant will be primarily responsible for the development of the classroom management program and for providing the teachers with a conceptual understanding of the procedures involved.

Goals of Consultation

The primary goal of the consultation is to train teachers in classroom management skills to such an extent that they will not only be able to provide remedial help to problem students in their current classrooms, but also will be able to develop remedial procedures for problem students in their future classes. During the training process the consultation will provide remedial services to behavioral problem students by reducing the occurrence of disruptive behaviors and increasing behaviors that will lead to better academic achievement.

Summary of the Classroom Management Program

The classroom management program has three basic features.

Classroom Observations: Classroom observation will be made for two weeks prior to the implementation of the point system as well as throughout the entire program. The observations will be conducted by the consultant at agreed upon times. During these periods, on-task and undesirable behaviors will be categorized and their frequencies recorded. Both the students and the teacher will be observed during each observation period. These observations are essential for providing objective information

The Role of the Consultant 13

concerning the types and degrees of disruption occurring in the classroom and the effect the program has on changing student behaviors.

Point System: As a result of the observations, basic categories of disruptive behaviors will be established. Classroom rules will then be established from these basic categories. The teacher will periodically rate each student on how well the student is following these rules. Points will be given to each student according to these ratings. The teacher will also periodically inform each student of desirable changes that occur in the student's behavior. Students who earn a specified number of points during the day will be eligible for an award.

Teacher-Student Interactions: The success of this program, particularly effective maintenance of the desirable student behaviors, depends upon the proper teacher interaction with the students. Consistency, shaping, and contingent praise will be practiced during the consultation sessions. Suggested teacher-student interaction guidelines will be provided.

The classroom management program serves five primary purposes:

1. It helps the teacher to keep track of how _each_ student is performing, both academically and behaviorally.
2. It provides an opportunity for the teacher and each student to interact in a positive manner each classroom day.
3. It provides the structure within which the teacher can learn to act as an effective reinforcer.
4. It provides information to the student about how well he or she is progressing each day.
5. It provides a means of recognizing and motivating each student's progress.

Teachers who may be interested in participating in the consultation should contact their school principal or the consultant, (consultant's name), at (the consultant's phone number).

Chapter 2

NEGOTIATIONS

CONSULTATION with a teacher may result from a school's request to an agency outside the school system, from a proposal addressed to a school by a consultant, or from the consultative responsibilities of personnel within the school system. Regardless of how the consultation is initiated, however, agreements concerning the purpose, conditions, and limitations of the consultation must be made with the principal and teacher during the initial contacts. In some instances, negotiations may involve district superintendents, those with responsibilities for specific school activities, or others who may be able to help arrange the consultation.

The consultant's major concern during these initial contacts is to establish a *mutually* cooperative working relationship with the teacher and principal. Clear understandings and agreements among the participants are, of course, the basis for cooperation during the consultation. All persons involved must first agree on what is to be accomplished — the purpose of the consultation. To set the conditions of the consultation, the consultant should next describe what is needed to provide consultation and what the responsibilities are of each participant. The limitations of the consultation, factors that affect the outcome of the consultation or that may result in its termination, should also be discussed. Agreements about these issues will provide a common frame of reference within which consultation can effectively occur. Early agreements also reduce the possibility of later disputes and misconceptions. Failure to reach agreement on essential points may indicate a need to modify the objectives of the consultation or perhaps may indicate that consultation cannot proceed at all. It is the consultant's responsibility to present these and other important issues for discussion, clarification, and negotiation during the initial meetings.

The Purpose of the Consultation

During the first meetings, the purpose of the consultation should be presented in terms of its benefits to the school. These benefits generally are the enhancement of teacher skills and the remediation of problem student behaviors. A teacher skilled in the classroom management of student behaviors will not only be beneficial to students in current and subsequent classes but also will be a resource for other teachers in the school. When discussing these benefits, the consultant should also briefly present the behavioral concepts upon which the consultation is based, the goals of teacher problem solving skills, and the goals for student behavior changes — all of which will be examined in detail later in the consultation. Here it should be emphasized that the consultant *assists the teacher* in developing and applying problem solving skills. The teacher maintains responsibility for the students in the classroom.

The Conditions for Consultation

The next topic of discussion during early meetings is the conditions under which consultation will be provided. This discussion should result in agreement about the teacher's participation, the responsibilities of the participants, and the resources that are available to support the teacher's efforts.

The teacher, it must be made clear, should participate voluntarily. Effective consultation cannot be provided to a teacher who does not want it. When obligated by the principal to participate, the teacher may eventually say, "Okay, all right, fine," but the enthusiasm and personal involvement necessary for an earnest effort may not be there. The teacher may in fact wish to prove that the consultant cannot do any better in managing student problems. There are numerous reasons a teacher may be reluctant to participate — suspicion that the consultant will evaluate the teacher for the principal, resentment based on the implication that the consultant knows more, a belief that the amount of time and work required will be too great, or the feeling that his or her authority in the classroom will be undermined. Many of these doubts and fears can be resolved by clarifying the conditions under which a teacher participates in the consultation.

It should be made clear that the consultant does not make evaluations of the teacher for the principal or address conflicts between the teacher and principal. The consultant should also describe his or her area of expertise and stress that the consultant's skills supplement rather than duplicate the expertise of the teacher. The consultant might define his or her area of expertise as the management of problem student behaviors and the teacher's as the fostering of student academic abilities. The teacher should be aware that participation will initially involve additional time and effort. It should also be emphasized that the teacher maintains all the responsibility and authority in the classroom. Again, it should be made explicit to both the teacher and principal that no one is obliged to participate. If the teacher does decide to participate, a commitment should be made to that decision.

With these preliminary but crucial considerations out of the way, the responsibilities of the teacher, principal, and consultant are the next issues to be discussed and agreed upon. Typical teacher responsibilities include attending meetings, preparing for meetings (completing readings, compiling records, drawing up charts), consistently following agreed upon procedures, and fulfilling school responsibilities concerning lesson plans, records, and school policies. Typical consultation responsibilities for a principal include ensuring that the teacher remains in the same class during the consultation, maintaining a stable student population in the class, recognizing teacher efforts, and carrying out administrative responsibilities involving parental consent and videotape releases. The consultant's responsibilities include the development of teacher skills, training the teacher to implement procedures for managing student behaviors, making classroom observations, and evaluating progress with the teacher.

In addition, the participants in the consultation must also agree upon the necessary resources for the support of the consultation, resources such as a meeting room, money to purchase reinforcers, supplementary instructional materials, films, the use of the gym or library, and other needed space or materials.

The Limitations on the Consultation

Consultation is not a guaranteed cure for student behavior problems; rather, it is an interactive process. Thus, the effectiveness of the consultation, both in the development of teacher skills and the desirable changes in student behaviors, may be limited by numerous factors. Many of these, implied under the conditions for consultation, can be anticipated and should be discussed to avoid misunderstandings. A major factor is the teacher's responsibility as the primary implementer of behavioral procedures in the classroom; the teacher largely determines the success or failure of the consultation. Adequate preparation of lessons and instructional materials by the teacher is essential to the remediation of problem student behaviors.

A second factor influencing the success of consultation is the matter of expectations. Both teacher and principal should have realistic expectations, recognizing that changes in problem student behaviors occur gradually and may require much time and effort from the teacher. The anticipated length of the consultation should be discussed and a meeting schedule and classroom observation schedule established. It should also be understood that there will be regularly scheduled times during the process of consultation when its productivity will be assessed. These times will permit discussion of any factors limiting the effectiveness of the consultation and will provide an opportunity for the teacher or consultant to withdraw from the consultation if it is assessed as unproductive.

Teacher Concerns

Below are a number of concerns teachers may express during negotiations. Their questions and their reactions to the consultant's responses are important indicators of how cooperative the teacher will ultimately be and, thus, how successful the consultation will be. It is extremely important that the consultant honestly, accurately, yet diplomatically respond to the concerns of the teacher in order to establish the teacher's confidence and cooperation. The topics covered in the negotiations should provide the bases for the consultant to reply to a teacher's doubts and concerns.

1. *Were you ever a teacher? I've taught for X number of years.* No, you (the teacher) are the expert in academic achievement, instructional materials, lesson plans, and educational theory. The consultant has skills in dealing with problem behaviors and has consulted with numerous teachers in many different classrooms.
2. *My students come from bad homes and a troubled community. How can I expect them to behave in the classroom when nothing is done for them at home?* Frequently students are not well prepared at home for appropriate classroom behaviors, so they must be taught these behaviors. Appropriate behaviors learned in the classroom might then generalize to the home.
3. *The problems of the students or class are not my (the teacher's) fault.* The problems of the students may not be the fault of the classroom teacher; however, they still must be dealt with by the teacher. Perhaps the consultant can be of assistance. The teacher's education emphasized skills to promote academic achievement; the consultant's education emphasized skills in the remediation of problem behaviors. These skills should complement each other.
4. *The student needs intensive therapy. What can you do for him? Where can I refer him?* The consultant does not take direct referrals but can suggest facilities that may be able to help. The consultant can make an initial assessment to determine whether the problem can be dealt with in the classroom by the teacher with the assistance of the consultant.
5. *The amount of time involved in the consultation project is too great; I need this time to teach.* The amount of time and work involved in the consultation is considerable but tapers down rather quickly. In the past, teachers have reported that

after they gained control over the problem behaviors, they spent less time on discipline and more on instruction. The students rate of academic achievement also increased as a result of their better behavior. However, you must consider the amount of time and work involved before making a commitment to participate in the consultation.
6. *The principal and I don't get along.* The purpose of the consultation is to provide the teacher with skills to deal with problem behaviors and is not to evaluate the teacher. No evaluation of the teacher will be made for the principal. The principal will be informed (as agreed to in the negotiations) of the procedures incorporated in the treatment plan and of the success in implementating the treatment plan. It is assumed, of course, that the principal will continue to make his or her own evaluation of the teaching staff in the same manner as in the past.

These examples obviously do not cover all possible teacher concerns. They do, however, represent ways in which many of the teacher's questions can be anticipated and addressed in the initial negotiation meetings.

At the conclusion of the negotiations, the principal should have sanctioned the consultation and the teacher should be committed to participate. A written agreement best emphasizes the understandings and responsibilities of the principal, teacher, and consultant. Failure to reach agreements on points considered essential by the consultant may indicate a need for modifying the objectives of the consultation or perhaps may indicate that consultation cannot proceed. Following the first meeting, a schedule for the consultant to meet with the teacher and a schedule for the consultant to observe in the classroom should both be drawn up. The meeting schedule might include two one-hour meetings per week, meetings preferably held outside the classroom but not during lunch. The object here is to avoid unnecessary distractions. The classroom observation schedule might include two to five one-hour classroom observations per week. The observations should be made at the same time each day, preferably in the afternoon when classrooms tend to be the most disrupted. The frequency of the observations depends on how much information must be given the teacher and how much data must be collected concerning changes in both teacher and student behaviors. Videotapes are often an effective means of providing such information to the teacher. According to school regulations, parents should be notified of the consultation.

An example of written agreements, a sample letter notifying parents about the consultation, and a consent form for videotaping follow.

AGREEMENTS

In order to maximize the likelihood of success of the consultation, the various participants identified below agree to carry out the following responsibilities to the best of their ability for the duration of the consultation.

I. The responsibilities of the consultant are the following:
   1. Design the classroom management program and explain its concepts to the teacher involved.
   2. Provide instruction and consultation to the teacher regarding implementation of the program.
   3. Make periodic videotape recordings of the classroom if needed for purposes of information and training.
   4. Conduct classroom observations on an average of four hours per week.
   5. Prepare for and participate in weekly meetings to provide information and instruction to the teacher.
   6. Purchase tangible reinforcers for use in the classroom.
   7. Keep the school principal informed regarding the status of the classroom program, avoiding reports or evaluations of teacher performance.
   8. Maintain involvement in the program until its completion, or as otherwise agreed upon during interim assessments.

II. Responsibilities of the classroom teacher will be as follows:
   1. Function as primary implementer of the classroom management program.
   2. Consistently follow guidelines established for teacher-student interactions.
   3. Prepare and maintain necessary charts, records, and forms.
   4. Prepare for and participate in weekly consultation sessions.
   5. Be in attendance in the classroom on a regular, uninterrrupted

basis.

6. Inform the consultant in advance of anticipated absences.
7. Continue to follow school policies and carry out required school responsibilities.
8. Be responsible for all lesson planning and classroom academic instruction.

III. The responsibilities of the school and its principal will be the following.

1. Maintain the teacher in her present classroom assignment.
2. Maintain stable student enrollment in classroom.
3. Provide funds to be used for the purchase of tangible reinforcers.
4. Make available, insofar as feasible, school resources and facilities for recognition of student behavioral improvements, e.g. gym, recess, library time, filmstrips.
5. Recognize and support the commitment of time and effort by the teacher.

Signed:

| Classroom Teacher | School Principal | Consultant |

| Date | Date | Date |

Sample Letter to Parents

Dear Parent:

As part of my continuing effort to improve the learning experience of my students, I am working on a classroom project with the assistance of (consultant's name), a consultant from (school or agency name). As part of this program, students who show improvement in their classroom work and behavior during the next two weeks may bring home awards they have earned. After the next two weeks, I will send notes to let you know about the times your child has shown improvement. I hope that you will praise your child when he or she brings home the awards or notes earned. Your continuing support of your child's work will greatly help my efforts.

Thank you for your interest. Please contact me if you have any questions.

Sincerely,

_____
Teacher

CONSENT TO VIDEOTAPE

Part of the services of the (school or agency name) is to assist teachers in developing classroom management skills that will enhance the learning experiences of their students. This assistance involves the videotaping of the teacher and students in their classroom. These videotapes will be viewed by teachers as part of their training.

Your child's teacher has given his/her consent to videotape in the classroom. We would also appreciate your consent to videotape the classroom your child is attending. We wish to thank you for your cooperation. Please sign below to indicate your consent.

_____   _____
Teacher   Date

_____   _____
Parent or Guardian   Date

Chapter 3

BEHAVIORAL PRINCIPLES

SINCE behavioral consultation focuses on the establishment of desirable student behaviors, much of the emphasis of the consultation is placed on the development of procedures to promote desired behavior changes. Unfortunately, the teacher whose exposure to behavioral principles is limited to that implied by specific procedures may come to view these procedures as little more than the means to control only those behavior problems addressed during consultation. Without a broader conceptual understanding of behavioral principles, the teacher may not have a sufficient basis for developing the procedures to resolve new problems or to assess the effectiveness of the procedures utilized. It thus becomes important for the teacher to gain a thorough understanding of the basic principles undergirding the procedures for changing student behaviors. In other words, the teacher must not only know what to do but why. The following subjects are introduced to assist the consultant in clarifying those behavioral principles for the teacher:

problems as behaviors
behaviors as learned
the changing of behaviors
the teacher as a change agent

Problems as Behaviors

It should be clearly understood that the problems addressed during consultation are the observable behaviors of students. Concern for students may be expressed in various ways. A teacher may identify a student, several students, or even an entire class as socially maladjusted, mentally handicapped, or having poor conduct. When exploring why the teacher has come to one of these conclusions, the consultant is likely to be told that the behaviors of the students have indicated that there is a problem. In describing what the student does, the teacher may state that the student acts crazy, clowns around a lot, is hyperactive, passive, aggressive, or defiant. The teacher may indicate that he or she has observed the student behaving in this way many times — "I have seen him running around the room, acting crazy, saying objectionable things. When asked to get to work, he doesn't pay any attention or becomes defiant, saying things like 'I won't, make me. Your Mama looks like she got hit in the face by a bag of nuts!' He's not very stable. Even little things will set him off. I'm concerned about his social adjustment." The basis for deciding that the student "has a problem" originated in the way the student behaves, how he acts, and what he says. The student is not the problem; the student's behavior is the problem.

Problem behaviors are those behaviors that someone wants to change or believes should be changed. Problems occur when there are differences between the way a person behaves and the way he is expected to behave. If the way the student behaves — what he does and what he says — is changed, the evidence for deciding that the student has a problem is changed and thus a reassessment of the problem is in order. Many teachers believe that a problem remains even after the student's problem behaviors have been corrected. "Even if the student's behaviors are changed," teachers often argue, "the student's feelings, emotions, and thoughts may not have changed." When exploring why the teacher has attributed certain feelings, emotions, or thoughts to the student, the consultant may find that the teacher has based these assumptions on an interpretation of previously observed student behaviors. Thus, the consultant must stress that the basis for deciding that the student has a problem is changed when the student's behaviors are changed. Behavioral consultation facilitates changes in behaviors.

Behaviors and inferences about behaviors are frequently confused. Since, from a behavioral perspective, behaviors are the targets for change, it is functionally important to make and maintain a distinction between "behaviors" and "inferences" about behaviors. *Behaviors* are the activities of a person —

what he does or says — that can be observed and thus measured in terms of frequency, duration, and intensity. A statement identifying a behavior should be precise so that it can serve as a unit of measurement for an observer to reliably record the occurrence of that behavior. Inferences about a behavior generally refer to the inner states of a person as the reason for that person's particular behavior. Inferences tend to be broad categorical statements, which include more than the behaviors that were observed. For example, a student may be labeled as phobic because he cries, defiant because he doesn't comply with requests, or hyperactive because he gets into frequent fights. Frequently, inferences serve as labels for a category of behaviors that may include different behaviors depending upon who is doing the inferring. Thus inferences cannot be reliably measured or observed.

Inferences are interpretations of what the behavior of a person means or indicates and are attributed by the observer to the person being observed. For example, a statement such as "The student gets out of his seat and runs around the classroom ten times a day" describes the student's behavior and can be reliably observed and verified. The number of times the student gets out of his seat and runs around the room can be counted and thus serve as a unit of measurement. An inference about this student's behavior might be "he is hyperactive," implying that he runs around the room because he is hyperactive. Yet playing with a book at one's desk, tapping one's feet, rocking in a seat, or throwing objects across the room may also indicate hyperactivity, depending on the interpretation of the meaning of "hyperactivity." The student, in actuality, may engage in some, none, or all of these behaviors. Thus, it becomes difficult to reliably observe and verify whether a student is hyperactive when hyperactivity is not clearly defined in behavioral terms. Hyperactivity cannot be changed without specifying and changing the behaviors that were observed and that led to the observer's inference that the student was hyperactive. To assess behavior by inference is to reason in a circle. To label a student hyperactive could imply that the student's behavior — getting out of his seat and running around — is caused by his hyperactivity and that he is hyperactive because he gets out of his seat and runs around the room.

Verbalizations are also measurable behaviors. Take for example a student who says "I won't do it." This verbalization, as well as others that are of concern to the teacher, can be measured in terms of frequency and intensity. However, an inference that this student is "defiant towards authority" or is "expressing inner hostility" or has a "negative attitude towards school" cannot be observed or measured unless these inferences have been defined operationally to mean that the student makes statements like "I won't do it." Certainly inferences about a person's behavior may be useful. The point here, however, is that in order to remedy a problem, the problem must be defined in terms of observable and measurable behaviors. Inferences are not behaviors being observed; they are interpretations made by the observer about the behaviors observed.

Behaviors as Learned

Behavioral principles are based on the premise that behaviors are learned through the interactions a person has with his or her environment. Any environment provides numerous stimuli for an individual. These stimuli have both tangible and social features that cue and act as consequences for a person's behavior. In the classroom, tangible features might include the arrangement of the desks and chairs and the presence of books and instructional material, paper and pencils, charts posted on the walls, and assignments written on the board. Social features might include verbal and nonverbal communication with the teacher and other students — smiles, greetings, tones of voice, attention, praise, and criticism — that convey approval or disapproval, acceptance or rejection, like or dislike. In a given situation, environmental stimuli cue a person to behave in a particular manner. For example, stimuli present on the school playground (swings, slides, monkey bars, other children playing games and laughing) may cue a child to behave in one manner while the stimuli present in the school library (shelves filled with books, the librarian, quiet signs, other children sitting and reading quietly) may cue a child to behave in a very different manner.

Environmental stimuli also function as consequences of a person's behavior. In a given situation, different behaviors by a person may produce different consequences. Playing in the library would probably result in a much different consequence than would reading quietly. Generally, a person learns to behave in a manner that results in physical and/or social comfort or in the avoidance or escape from physical and/or social discomfort. Thus, to change a behavior, the environmental stimuli that act as cues and consequences for a person's behavior must be changed.

Consequences that determine if a behavior will be learned, maintained, or changed may be neutral, reinforcing, or punishing in their effects on the behavior that then immediately follows. A *neutral* consequence of a behavior neither facilitates the acquisition of something that is desired nor the avoidance of or escape from something that is aversive. Since a person's behaviors are generally purposeful, behaviors that are followed by a neutral consequence tend to decrease or extinguish. There are two types of reinforcing consequences, positive and negative reinforcement. Both of these reinforcing consequences result in an *increase* in the probability that the behavior they follow will occur again. It should be noted that a reinforcer is defined by its effect on behavior, not by its intent. A reinforcer is only a reinforcer if the behavior that it follows increases.

Positive reinforcement occurs when a person's behavior results in the acquisition of or coming closer to the acquisition of something that he or she desires. A person tends to learn and engage in those behaviors that result in something that the person perceives as desirable. *Negative reinforcement* occurs when a person's behavior results in the termination of something that the person perceives as aversive or undesirable. A person tends to learn and engage in those behaviors that result in the termination, avoidance, or escape from aversive stimuli. There are also two types of punishing consequences. Both types of punishment result in a *decrease* in the probability that the behavior that they follow will occur again. *Punishment* occurs when the behavior of a person is followed by the presentation of an aversive stimulus or the removal of a positive reinforcer. A person tends not to engage in those behaviors that result in something that the person perceives as undesirable.

	To **increase** a behavior	To **decrease** a behavior
Positive Reinforcer	PRESENTATION (positive reinforcement)	REMOVAL (punishment)
Aversive Stimulus	REMOVAL (negative reinforcement)	PRESENTATION (punishment)
Neutral		EXTINCTION

As a person comes in contact with the consequences of his or her behavior in a given situation, environmental stimuli present in that situation come to be associated with those consequences. In some situations environmental stimuli may be associated with reinforcing events while in other situations they may be associated with punishing events. Through this association these stimuli acquire cueing properties that signal a person to behave in a particular manner. Similar situations are likely to cue a person to behave in similar manners because of the presence of environmental stimuli that have previously been associated with reinforcing or punishing events. Environmental stimuli present in a situation cue a person to behave or not to behave in manners that have been reinforced or punished in similar past situations. For example, a student who has frequently been praised (a positive reinforcer) by the teacher for starting his classwork (the behavior) as soon as he comes into the classroom (the situation) learns to associate starting work immediately after coming into the classroom with teacher praise. The stimuli present in the classroom — the presence of the teacher, the assignment written on the board, other students working — act as cues for the student to start his classwork. Thus, the situation both cues a person's behavior by the presence of familiar environmental stimuli and directs a person's behavior by selectively reinforcing or punishing different behaviors.

The Changing of Behaviors

Since behaviors are a function of their consequences, behaviors can be changed by changing the consequences that follow a behavior in a given situation. In the classroom, for example, a student who yells out "Hey teacher!" to gain the teacher's attention may be reinforced for yelling out (the behavior) by the teacher's reply of "I'll be there in a minute!" (a positive reinforcer). If the teacher desires to change the student's behavior, the consequence of the student's behavior should be changed. Instead of being followed by a positive reinforcer, the student's yelling could be ignored, the teacher could cue the student to the proper way of gaining his or her attention by asking the class, "Who knows what to do to get my attention?" or the student's yelling could be followed by an aversive consequence.

To change a student's behavior there are two behaviors that must be specified, the undesirable or problem behavior to be decreased and the desirable behavior to be increased. Whenever possible, emphasis should be placed on increasing desirable behaviors to replace the undesirable behaviors rather than focusing solely on decreasing the undesirable behaviors. Exceptions to this rule of thumb would include behaviors that may be injurious to the student or others, behaviors that involve destruction of property, and behaviors that are extremely disruptive to the functioning of the class. Because of the serious nature of these behaviors, direct action is often required to stop their occurrence immediately.

Since behaviors occur continuously, it is not possible to remove a problem behavior without replacing that behavior with another behavior. In order to reduce the possibility of a problem behavior being replaced by another problem behavior, a desirable behavior that is incompatible with the occurrence of the problem behavior should be specified and reinforced. For example, if out of one hour of class time, a student spends a half hour working on the class assignment and the remaining half hour running around the room, the objective is not solely to eliminate running around the room, even if it were successfully eliminated, there would still be a half hour for the student to engage in other possibly undesirable behaviors, such as sleeping or daydreaming. An assessment should be made of what behaviors the student should be engaged in during that half hour. The solution might be to increase the amount of time the student attends to the class assignment, or, if the assignment is finished, he or she might do extra credit work, work on an art project, or help the teacher. Emphasizing desirable behaviors provides opportunities for the student to earn positive reinforcers in a productive manner and provides the student with a direction in which to change behaviors.

When establishing desirable behaviors, a distinction should be made between teaching new behaviors and increasing the frequency of behaviors that are already learned but occurring too infrequently. Teaching new behaviors involves shaping and modeling. In *shaping* a behavior, the behavior is broken down into small steps. Gradual improvement — the achieving of each of the steps — is then reinforced. The criteria for reinforcement are gradually increased until all the steps of the behavior have been sequentially learned. For example, a student who does not know how to do math might be reinforced for attempting to do math, then for doing a math problem correctly, then for doing several problems, and so on until he or she is reinforced for completing the assignment. *Modeling* involves demonstrating what the behavior to be learned looks like. Demonstrating the behavior to the student should clarify the steps involved in the behavior expected from the student.

To increase the frequency of a learned but low-frequency behavior, the reinforcing consequences of that behavior must be increased beyond the reinforcing consequences of the undesirable behavior that it is to replace. An example of this would be a student who spends time drawing instead of doing math, even though he or she knows how to do the math. Here the consequence of drawing must be more reinforcing to the student than the consequence of doing math. The solution is to make the consequence of doing math relatively more reinforcing. This may involve recognition and praise for the student's math ability, giving the student more challenging math assignments, having the student help other students after finishing the assignment, or allowing him or her to draw after finishing the math. It should be noted that it is generally preferable to change a behavior by the use of positive reinforcement than by punishment. The aversive effects resulting from the excessive use of punishment may generalize to being in the classroom and result in the student's desire to avoid or escape that situation. The students may also acclimate to the punishment, requiring the teacher to continually increase the intensity of the punisher. Though punishment can counteract the reinforcers that are maintaining a problem behavior, punishers should be used sparingly. Emphasis should be placed on making desirable behaviors more reinforcing.

Changing student behaviors involves changing the relationship between the student's behavior and its consequences. The relationship between a person's behavior and its consequences are described in terms of contingencies. *Contingencies* are essentially "if-then" statements. *If* a student behaves in a specified manner, *then* a specified consequence will immediately follow. Changes in contingent relationships involve the restructuring of the reinforcing consequences that follow various behaviors in a given situation. Reinforcers for desirable behaviors are made available, and reinforcers for undesirable behaviors are removed. The students should be aware of the behaviors expected of them. Explicit instructions and modeling of the behaviors that are expected of the student should be provided. The reinforcing consequences of engaging in these behaviors should also be stated by the teacher. Other cues, such as posters of classroom rules and periodic verbal reminders from the teacher, should be provided to remind the students of the desired behaviors. Consistency is very important. Behaviors are learned through the *consistent* recurrence of the contingent relationship between a behavior and its consequences. Behaviors change gradually as a person continues to experience the consistent contingent relationship between his or her behavior and its consequences in a given situation. Teacher praise, attention, and recognition should consistently follow desirable student behaviors and gradual improvements in student behaviors. The teacher must be able to assess contingent relationships between problem behaviors and their consequences and know how to structure them in a manner that will reinforce desirable student behaviors.

The Teacher as a Change Agent

Behavioral principles describe how behaviors are learned, maintained, and changed by the interactions an individual has with his or her environment. The environment is always providing cues and consequences that influence a person's behavior, whether or not the environment is intentionally structured to do so. It is important to recognize that behavioral principles describe how the environment, consisting of a multitude of stimuli that vary from situation to situation, continually affects a person's behavior. Understanding these principles can assist a teacher in changing his or her own behaviors in a manner that will favorably influence the behavior of the students. Changes in student behaviors involve the restructuring, by the teacher, of the cues and consequences provided in the classroom environment.

Behavioral principles themselves do not indicate which behaviors are desirable and which are undesirable. In the classroom, the teacher assesses student behaviors and decides what behaviors are or are not acceptable. The teacher's assessment (in terms of grades, promotions, demotions, honor rolls, and disciplinary actions) determines a student's progress through school; however, it is not sufficient for the teacher solely to assess student behaviors. Students cannot be expected to fulfill the teacher's expectations unless the teacher provides a classroom environment that is conducive to developing the student behaviors that are desired. A teacher may have students in the class who have not previously learned the behaviors that the teacher assesses as desirable. These students must be taught desirable classroom behaviors. The teacher must structure cues and consequences that teach problem students the behaviors expected of them, rather than leave the remediation of their problem behaviors to chance.

Changing a student's behavior requires the teacher to change his or her own behavior. The teacher must learn how to establish and maintain desirable student behaviors. The teacher must continually monitor his or her own behaviors to ensure that cueing and reinforcing desirable behaviors and following through with contingencies established for developing desirable student behaviors are consistently carried out. The teacher must establish himself or herself as a positive reinforcer for desirable student behaviors. In the classroom, the teacher is the primary environmental stimulus affecting student behaviors. It is the teacher's responsibility to plan not only how the students should behave but also what to do to facilitate the development of desirable student behaviors. With the assistance of the consultant, the teacher must develop skills in the management of student behaviors. To a large extent, what the teacher does or does not do will determine what a student does or does not do while in the classroom.

Teacher Concerns

Following are representative concerns teachers may express during the review of the behavioral principles. The subjects covered in the review should provide a basis for the consultant to reply to these concerns. It is important that the consultant present the behavioral principles in a manner that is acceptable and satisfying to the teacher and with as little dogmatism as possible. It is helpful to illustrate the principles with practical *classroom* examples. Based on the consultant's assessment of how satisfactorily the teacher's concerns are met during both the negotiations and review of the principles, the consultant may decide to terminate or continue the consultation.

Replies to the concerns presented below are meant as guidelines, not as complete or even adequate replies; from these the consultant can develop replies while drawing upon examples based on the context of the concern and the consultant's own experiences.

1. *You're only dealing with behaviors and not emotions.* Emotions are inferred from behaviors. If a student's behaviors are changed, the basis for making inferences about a student's emotions is changed. The goal of a behavioral approach is to provide a classroom environment in which students will enjoy learning. Doing this will benefit a student's emotional as well as behavioral development.
2. *You're only addressing symptoms (specific behaviors) and not dealing with the basic cause of the student's actions.* The assumption of a behavioral approach is that the environment is the basic cause of a person's behavior. Changing behaviors involves the restructuring of the individual's environment. When a desirable behavior is established that replaces a problem behavior, there is no evidence that symptom substitution occurs. However, a student may have several problem behaviors that may need to be corrected.
3. *Children should behave because it's the right thing to do, not because I'm paying them off. They should like to learn.* The students are currently getting payoffs for being disruptive. It is better to structure the class so that the students can *earn* reinforcers based on their achievements. The goal is that the students eventually will not need this high degree of structure or the explicit reinforcers. They can be removed when learning itself becomes reinforcing to the student. Contingencies are used to facilitate the effectiveness of social reinforcers and to develop student self-control.
4. *Is it fair to my class to have special programs for certain children?* In the same manner that you make allowances for individual differences in academic subjects like reading and math, you can allow for individual differences in behaviors. Furthermore, it does not seem fair to either the disruptive students or the other students to allow disruptive behaviors to continue.
5. *You can't expect me to reinforce good behaviors all the time when there are thirty students in my class.* Initially the time and effort required of the teacher is great but this diminishes as the teacher's skills develop and the students' behaviors

improve. Lessening problem student behaviors will reduce the amount of time the teacher may have to spend attending to problem behaviors.
6. *Punishment works very well and is more effective than when I try positive reinforcement.* The use of punishment is probably uncomfortable for the teacher who continually uses it. The intensity of the punishment must be continually increased in order for it to remain effective. Thus, the teacher, the school, and learning may become aversive to the students, resulting in avoidance and escape behaviors. Punishment does not teach the students what to do; it only teaches them what not to do.
7. *I've tried reinforcing students with cookies, stars, etc. and it didn't work for very long.* The novelty of these tangible reinforcers may have worn off before reinforcers that are more natural to the classroom environment became effective. The selection of the reinforcers, the contingencies, and the context in which the reinforcers were given, all influence the effectiveness of a reinforcer. The reinforcers for disruptive behaviors may have been greater than the reinforcer offered for good behavior. Conditioned reinforcers that are natural to the classroom setting, such as teacher praise, grades, and peer recognition, should have been established.
8. *I would like the students to be able to learn from each other in an open classroom setting.* This is a desirable objective; however, students need to learn prerequisite behaviors first — behaviors such as self-control, learning on their own, and cooperation — before they can be expected to learn in an open classroom.

An understanding of behavioral principles provides the foundation for developing classroom management procedures. Discussion of these principles should facilitate the development of specific management procedures by providing an understanding of how these procedures are derived. A mutual understanding of the terms to be used and the objectives of the consultation should also be established. Once a conceptual basis for the consultation is established, the steps involved in the problem solving process begin.

Part II
Problem Solving

The efficacy of the behavioral principles presented in Chapter 3 has long been recognized. Applied to a variety of classrooms by many different teachers and consultants, these principles have been the basis for numerous successful programs for the remediation of problem student behaviors and the establishment of desirable ones. The ultimate success of these programs has always depended heavily on the classroom teacher; after all, they are the most important mediators of the many environmental stimuli governing student actions. Using reasonable discretion, the teacher defines what student behaviors are "desirable" and "undesirable" and decides how these desirable behaviors are to be established. The problem, however, lies in the discrepancy between what the teacher defines as desirable student behaviors and the teacher's skills in establishing and maintaining these student behaviors. It is the consultant's responsibility to develop these teacher skills. Desirable changes in student behaviors will not occur until the teacher is able to create an environment that will foster these changes. Thus, the overall objective is not for the consultant to resolve the behavior problems of the students, but for the teacher to develop the skills necessary to apply the problem solving process. Only in this way will the teacher ever be consistently able to alter problem student behaviors. The problem solving steps presented in Chapters 4 through 10 of Part II correspond to the development of the teacher's skills in the following areas:

Chapter 4. Specifying Problem Student Behaviors

Chapter 5. Assessing Problem Student Behaviors

Chapter 6. Measuring Behaviors

Chapter 7. Specifying Desirable Student Behaviors

Chapter 8. Identifying Positive Reinforcers

Chapter 9. Specifying Contingent Relationships

Chapter 10. Developing Positive Teacher-Student Interactions

Chapter 11. A Classroom Management Program, presents a sample program — procedures and forms that integrate the information gathered during the problem solving process.

Chapter 4

SPECIFYING PROBLEM STUDENT BEHAVIORS

PROBLEM student behaviors are behaviors viewed by another, usually the teacher, as undesirable. The first step in resolving a problem is to specify what that problem is. With problem student behaviors it is the *occurrence* of the undesired behaviors that is the problem. In other words, before these behaviors can be dealt with, they must first be specified in terms of observable behaviors that the student(s) actually engages in. Once specified, problem student behaviors become those behaviors targeted to be decreased or eliminated. At this point in the consultation, the function of the consultant is to assist the teacher to specify the problem student behaviors by changing the terms used to describe the problems from general, subjective labels to descriptions of observable behaviors actually occurring in the classroom.

Labeling

Generally, the teacher gives an initial description of problems early in the consultation. When describing the problems, however, a teacher may tend to label students rather than describe their actual behaviors. For example, the teacher might apply such labels as hyperactive, defiant, indifferent, inattentive, instigator, troublemaker, class clown, underachiever, disruptive, or passive. With only these initial "descriptions" the consultant will find it very difficult to know what a student is actually doing. All the consultant can really tell is that the student is doing something that displeases the teacher. Labels do not specify observable student behaviors; rather, they reflect the teacher's interpretation of the students' behaviors.

The use of labels to identify student behaviors targeted for change often causes ambiguity. A label such as "hyperactivity" can vary in its application to include any number of behaviors. For one teacher, it may mean that the student does the work too quickly, carelessly, and sloppily. For another teacher, it may mean that the student talks constantly and fidgets at his or her desk a lot. Yet another teacher may interpret hyperactivity as meaning elements mentioned above and also that the student runs around the room screaming and shouting, throws objects, and gets into frequent fights. Another possible problem with the use of labels is that the behaviors implied by one label may overlap with the behaviors implied by another label. For example, the labels hyperactive, disruptive, and troublemaker may be used by a teacher to describe different behaviors of different students or may be used by different teachers to describe the same student. When labels are used to describe problem behaviors, the consultant and teacher may not have a mutual understanding of what the problem student behaviors actually are.

Predispositions

The teacher's specification of problem student behaviors is further complicated by his or her attitude toward a student. A teacher may perceive a student as the class clown, a troublemaker, hard working, creative, or mischievous. These perceptions may, in turn, influence a teacher's description of the behaviors of that student. Making a hat out of a milk carton might be viewed as creative, clowning around, or causing a disturbance depending on the student who made the hat and what the teacher's perception is of that student. Even though given in observable terms, the specification of problem behaviors may be influenced by the teacher's bias and may thus not be entirely accurate. Classroom observations made by the consultant are, therefore, useful for verifying the accuracy of and supplementing the teacher's specification of problem student behaviors. Classroom observations are further discussed in Chapter 6.

Behavioral Excesses

Problem student behaviors are behavioral excesses of a student. That is, a student is doing something that is viewed as undesirable or is doing something too frequently, too long, or too intensely. Fighting, swearing, destroying school property, and throwing objects in the classroom are examples of behaviors generally considered undesirable. With these behaviors, even one occurrence is viewed as excessive and thus it must be stopped. For other behaviors, there are acceptable levels at which they can occur. Exceeding that level is viewed as undesirable and the teacher may want the behavior to decrease. An example of this type of behavior is a student who talks too much and walks around the room all day. Certainly, students must talk and walk around. The problem here comes with "too much" and "all day." These qualities indicate that what the student is doing is excessive and should be decreased to an acceptable level. In both examples, the problem behaviors are behavioral excesses; that is, the student is *doing* something that he or she should not be doing.

Since problem student behaviors are behaviors that are occurring excessively, the consequences of these behaviors must be highly reinforcing to the student. After the problem student behaviors have been specified in terms of observable behaviors actually occurring in the classroom, then the reinforcing consequences maintaining the problem behaviors must be identified and an assessment made of the situations that may cue problem behaviors. In order to decrease or extinguish a behavior, the consequences of that behavior must be changed. The consequences of engaging in undesired behaviors must be made less reinforcing to the student than the consequences of engaging in the desired behaviors with which they compete.

Behavioral Deficits

When specifying student problems, a teacher may sometimes describe what the student is *not doing;* for example, "The problem is that the student never does his work, can't sit still, and doesn't know how to get along with other students." The behaviors of the student are not being described here. With this description, the consultant does not know what the student is doing but rather what the student is *not* doing and what the teacher would like the student to do. Problems described in such terms indicate behavioral deficits. Behavioral deficits are behaviors that are desired of the student but that have not been learned or are not sufficiently reinforcing to the student and, thus, are *not* engaged in by the student or are not occurring at the desired level. Though it is important to specify the desirable student behaviors to replace problem behaviors, a distinction should be maintained between problem student behaviors and desirable student behaviors, between behaviors to be decreased and behaviors to be increased. Specifying desirable student behaviors is discussed in Chapter 7.

A student is always engaged in a behavior whether that behavior is running, talking, sleeping, daydreaming, or working on art instead of math. When a student is *not* doing one thing, then he or she *must* be doing something else. It is important to identify what the student is doing when not doing what is desired of him or her. In discussing this topic with the teacher, however, the consultant should be sensitive to the concerns of the teacher as the teacher expresses them. Care should be taken not to alienate the teacher by discarding his or her expressions of student problems. Information concerning what the student does not do is, after all, useful for specifying the desirable student behaviors to replace the undesirable ones.

*Consultation Agenda**

The development of the teacher's skill in specifying problem student behaviors should result in the ability to specify actual

---

*The consultation agenda does not necessarily cover topics for *one* consultation session. Depending on the problems to be addressed, characteristics of both the teacher and consultant, and the intent of the consultation, the suggested agenda may be covered in only part of a session or may be covered during several sessions. This proviso holds true for other suggested agenda presented in the remaining chapters of part II.

problematic student behaviors that occur in the classroom and that correspond to the classroom observations made by the consultant. Developing this teacher skill includes providing the teacher with a rationale for identifying specific observable behaviors, asking the teacher for examples and clarifications of what the students are doing when they are problematic, observing the students in the classroom to verify and supplement the teacher's problem specification, and arriving at a mutually agreed upon problem list of the behaviors to be decreased. The following consultation agenda and example forms are suggested.

AGENDA

1. *Provide a definition of "problem student behaviors."* They are actual behaviors occurring in the classroom that the teacher perceives as undesirable and excessive.
2. *Discuss guidelines for and utility of specifying problem student behaviors.* This includes difficulties with labeling, predispositions, behavioral deficits, and problem behaviors as target behaviors to be decreased.
3. *Identify problem students and their behaviors that are of concern to the teacher.* Ask for examples and clarifications when concerns are not stated in terms of behaviors. Complex problems and multiple problem students may require the listing of components of the problems or interrelated problems in an order reflecting the teacher's concern. Identifying information and the problem behaviors as expressed by the teacher should be recorded for each target student on a student information sheet (see example sheet).
5. *Obtain the information necessary to make classroom observations.* This information includes a class schedule noting times specific subjects are taught and times the students are not in the classroom (see the sample) and a seating chart (see the example).
6. *Schedule a time to make classroom observations.* Classroom observations generally take about thirty minutes. They should be scheduled at a time when problem student behav-

iors are most likely to occur. There should be a place in the back of the room for the consultant to sit. The teacher should announce to the class that there will be a visitor in the room and that the students are not to disturb him or her.
7. *Make classroom observations.* Note the behaviors of students, both problematic and desirable behaviors. Take notes on possible cues and consequences, especially the teacher's responses to both problematic and desirable student behaviors (see the example of observation notes, Chapter 5 and Chapter 6). The consultant should not, in any manner, interact with the students while in the classroom. If the presence of the consultant becomes excessively disruptive, the consultant should leave.
8. *During the subsequent consultation session, the problem list should again be discussed with the teacher.* Revisions or supplements to the problem list may result from the classroom observations.

The primary question to be answered at this point of the consultation is "What are the students doing that displeases the teacher?"

STUDENT INFORMATION

Teacher _____ School _____ Phone # _____

Room # _____ Grade _____ # of Students ___

Consultation Beginning _____ Ending _____

Student _____ Sex _____ Birthdate _____

Parent _____ Address _____ Phone # _____

Problem Behaviors _____

Student _____ Sex _____ Birthdate _____

Parent _____ Address _____ Phone # _____

Problem Behaviors _____

Student _____ Sex _____ Birthdate _____

Parent _____ Address _____ Phone # _____

Problem Behaviors _____

Student _____ Sex _____ Birthdate _____

Parent _____ Address _____ Phone # _____

Problem Behaviors _____

Student _____ Sex _____ Birthdate _____

Parent _____ Address _____ Phone # _____

Problem Behaviors _____

CLASS SCHEDULE

Please record the subject being taught (reading, math, music, art, etc.), noting the times when the students will not be in the classroom by circling the activity ((lunch), (recess), (gym), (library), etc.)

	Mon.	Tues.	Wed.	Thurs.	Fri.
8:00					
8:30					
9:00					
9:30					
10:00					
10:30					
11:00					
11:30					
12:00					
12:30					
1:00					
1:30					
2:00					
2:30					
3:00					
3:30					
4:00					

Seating Chart

The following teacher record form will subsequently be used by the teacher for recording student behaviors. The boxes are arranged in six rows and six columns, reflecting the student desk arrangement in a typical classroom. This form can also be used as a seating chart by writing the appropriate student name on top of each box.

TEACHER RECORD

Observation Notes

The following form is used for recording descriptions of problematic student behaviors and teacher reactions to these behaviors as they are observed by the consultant in the classroom. These observations are made to verify and supplement the teacher's descriptions of problem student behaviors. Once verified, the problem behaviors become the targets for change during the consultation — the behaviors that are to be measured and recorded during the subsequent baseline and treatment observations. The observation notes are used during the initial observations to record who the problem students are, what they are doing, and how the teacher handles these problems.

OBSERVATION NOTES

Classroom:_____ Observer:_____

Date:_____ Time:_____ Subject:_____

Student Name	Student Behaviors	+ -	Teacher Behaviors

Comments:

Chapter 5

ASSESSING PROBLEM STUDENT BEHAVIORS

AN assessment of problem student behaviors involves, first of all, the identification of the cues and consequences that maintain those behaviors. Once identified, the consultant and teacher can determine whether these cues and consequences can be restructured or should be removed in order to decrease or extinguish the problem behaviors. The function of the consultant at this point in the consultation is to assist the teacher in assessing the environmental variables that may be contributing to the occurrence of the identified problem student behaviors.

Precipitating Conditions

When considering the origins of a particular behavior, the consultant must remember several things. A student learns behaviors — some of them in conflict with those expected by the teacher — in many different settings (at home, through neighborhood interactions with friends and other peers, through church affiliation, gang membership, the mass media, or subcultural expectations). A behavior may be a transient reaction to a stressful change in the student's life or may be a characteristic response that has developed from a long history of previous learning experiences. A behavior may also be physiological in origin and may need to be evaluated by an appropriately trained professional. All of these factors may influence the student's classroom behavior. When appropriate, the consultant should suggest the involvement of parents, physicians, or others who may be able to assist in assessment or facilitate desirable changes.

Regardless of where problem behaviors originated, however, the teacher is primarily responsible for changing those problem student behaviors that occur in the classroom. To do this, the classroom situation must be restructured. Though a student's behavior cannot be attributed solely to prevailing conditions in the classroom, many problem student behaviors can be changed in the classroom by the teacher. The teacher can provide a classroom environment — the cues and consequences — that will teach a problem student alternative desirable behaviors. A student can be taught to discriminate between how he or she should behave in the classroom and how he or she behaves in other settings. Desirable behaviors learned in the classroom may then generalize to other settings in the same manner that behaviors learned outside the classroom often occur in the classroom. It may not always be possible, however, to restructure or remove all of the precipitating conditions that contribute to the occurrence of problem behaviors, but the identification of these conditions will enable the teacher and consultant to determine more precisely what types of appropriate cues and consequences should be established in the classroom.

Classroom Cues and Consequences

A classroom assessment of problem student behaviors does not focus solely on what the student is doing. It also includes an assessment of the behaviors of the teacher and other students in the class as well as other classroom variables that may cue and follow problem student behaviors. What the teacher does, the behavior of other students, and the classroom setting itself continually influence the behavior of each student in the classroom. Cues that may set the occasion for problem behaviors in the classroom are many — inadequate instructions, inappropriate instructional material, time gaps between lessons, inconsistency in teacher behaviors, encouragement or teasing by other students, seating arrangements, a messy classroom, visitors coming into the room, or other distractions. Consequences that may be reinforcing and thus maintain problem behaviors include peer recognition, involvement in inappropriate but pleasurable activities, obtaining tangible items, avoiding aversive events, and receiving the teacher's attention. An assessment of problem student behaviors should identify contingent relationships between the student's behavior and the classroom cues that precede the behavior and the consequences that follow it.

It is, however, often difficult to identify specific classroom stimuli that act as cues and consequences for a student's behavior. For many behaviors, numerous interacting stimuli present in a given situation set the occasion for and provide the consequences of student behaviors. Consider the example of a student who has nothing to do. He notices an eraser on the floor near his desk. The teacher is busy writing the next lesson on the chalkboard. The student picks up the eraser. Another student sitting nearby smiles and points to a girl sitting across the room. The student throws the eraser, hitting the girl. The other students in the class giggle. The teacher turns and angrily asks, "Who threw that?" Several antecedent conditions that set the occasion for the problem behavior can be identified — the student had "nothing to do," an eraser was nearby, the teacher was busy, and the student was being encouraged by another student. Several possible reinforcing consequences for throwing the eraser can also be identified — the termination of having "nothing to do," peer recognition, and "getting the teacher's goat." Most of the cues and consequences in this example could be changed by a skilled teacher.

Teacher Behaviors

The teacher, as already suggested, plays a primary role in stimulating particular student behaviors. Characteristic teacher behaviors, what the teacher does or does not do in the classroom, act as cues and consequences for these behaviors. The assessment of problem student behaviors should, therefore, reveal ways the teacher could change his or her behaviors in order to effect desired changes in the student behaviors. The consultant is responsible for identifying teacher behaviors that may be contributing to the occurrence of undesirable student behaviors. The consultant is also responsible for providing the teacher with alternative ways of interacting with the students. In doing this, the consultant should emphasize the teacher's appropriate behaviors and identify those times when the teacher's behaviors helped establish and maintain desirable student behaviors. The consultant should, of course, avoid repetitive criticism of the teacher's methods of managing students. Instead, the consultant should note, whenever possible, desirable behaviors by the teacher and problem situations in which those desirable behaviors might be effective for managing other student behaviors.

In the example of the eraser throwing, there are several possible alternatives for the teacher to explore to correct the problem behavior. Having nothing to do was a major factor setting the occasion for the student to misbehave. The student may think that there is "nothing to do" having finished the assignment, not being able to do the assignment (it is too difficult, he does not know what to do, he forgot to bring the book, pencil, or paper), not wanting to do the assignment (it is too boring or too long, the student doesn't see any purpose in doing it, the student does not like the subject matter), or the student may be waiting for the teacher to finish putting the next assignment on the board. The teacher, however, could individualize assignments according to student abilities. Extra-credit work could be made available to students who finish early. Lessons could be planned and placed on the board well in advance. Instructional objectives could be provided to the students for each lesson. The teacher could attend to and provide frequent praise for student progress. Grades, activities, or honor roll charts could be used to recognize student accomplishments. Thus, an assessment of problem student behaviors should indicate ways in which the teacher should change his or her own behaviors.

Consultation Agenda

The following agenda and example forms are suggested for the consultant as he or she develops the teacher's behavioral assessment skills.

AGENDA

1. *Provide a rationale for assessing problem behaviors.* Precipitating conditions must be identified in order to correct them. If these conditions cannot be corrected, the teacher and consultant should still be aware of them when developing procedures to establish desirable behaviors.
2. *Discuss possible precipitating conditions that may exist outside the classroom setting.* These conditions may include home and community factors of concern to the teacher as well as possible physical or other medical impairments. Such conditions may require the involvement of parents, physicians, or others who can assist in assessment and subsequent treatment.
3. *Discuss possible classroom cues and consequences that may contribute to the occurrence of problem student behaviors.* This discussion should include the teacher's description of the context in which the problem occurs (e.g. time of day, subject being taught) and the teacher's perception of what the cues and consequences are that contribute to the occurrence of problem behaviors. The teacher's report of what he or she does in response to problem student behaviors should also be included.
4. *Establish a written assessment inventory listing the cues and consequences for the identified problem behaviors. (See* example of assessment inventory at the end of this chapter.) Several cues and consequences may be related to several different problem behaviors and thus may be noted in that manner on the assessment inventory.
5. *Make further classroom observations to verify and identify cues and consequences for student behaviors. Supplement or revise the assessment inventory accordingly.* In making the observation, the consultant should note the teacher's behaviors (does the teacher attend only to disruptive students, does the teacher provide adequate instructions, does the teacher circulate through the room to assist students), the behavior of other students in the class (does the identified problem student initiate problems, should the seating arrangement be

changed), and the physical condition of the classroom (is the classroom messy, are there books, materials, etc. that are easily accessible to students that may distract them)?

6. *Elicit from and provide the teacher with suggestions for alternative ways to correct the cues and consequences maintaining problem behaviors.* These may include removing classroom distractions, changing seating arrangements, or suggesting that the teacher respond to student behaviors in a different manner.

The primary question to be answered at this point of the consultation is "What are the classroom stimuli that are cueing and reinforcing problem student behaviors and what can be done to change them?"

ASSESSMENT INVENTORY

List the cues and consequences for each of the target behaviors and comment on the ways that they may be restructured.

Target Behavior:_____

Cues:_____
_____

Consequences:_____
_____

Comments:_____
_____

Target Behavior:_____

Cues:_____
_____

Consequences:_____
_____

Comments:_____
_____

Target Behavior:_____

Cues:_____
_____

Consequences:_____
_____

Comments:_____
_____

Chapter 6

MEASURING BEHAVIORS

THE purpose of making classroom observations is, initially, to identify and then to assess the student behaviors to be targeted for change. Once these behaviors have been specified in observable terms, they can be measured and an index of their severity obtained. Subsequent classroom observations by the consultant are primarily directed to the measurement of behaviors — the development and maintenance of a record keeping system, which the consultant uses to record the occurrence of problem student behaviors throughout the consultation. Such a record will provide an objective measure of the severity of problem behaviors and of changes that may result from efforts to remedy them. The consultant's function at this point in the consultation is to establish this record keeping system.

The Purpose of Measuring Behaviors

The measurement of behaviors serves several useful functions. The most apparent is that the recording of student behaviors provides a continuous and objective record of the effectiveness of efforts to change student behaviors. Also, these recordings offer the consultant an objective format for providing information to the teacher. Gradual decreases in problem student behaviors, which might not otherwise be perceived, can be noted. Furthermore, this recognition of desirable changes in student behaviors is a major source of reinforcement for the development of the teacher's student management skills. Finally, having this objective measure reduces the effects of the predispositions and desires of the teacher and consultant since the evaluation of changes in student behaviors and the effectiveness of the procedures utilized are not based solely on subjective criteria.

Recording Behaviors

The severity of problem behaviors is expressed in terms of frequency, duration, or intensity. Frequency, the number of times a problem behavior occurs during a specified length of time, is recorded on observation sheets (*see* the example of an observation sheet). When the frequency of a behavior is recorded, the occurrence of that observably specified behavior serves as the unit by which these behaviors are counted and recorded. To facilitate recordings during the observation period, target behaviors are generally recorded in codes (S = out of seat, N = making noise, etc.). Duration, the amount of time the behavior continues once it begins, and intensity, the forcefulness of the behavior when it occurs, can be reflected in the operational definition of each of the target behaviors ("out of seat for one minute or more" specifies duration; "making noise that disturbs two or more students" implies intensity). Observation periods are typically scheduled for one-half to one hour a day at the same time each day and at a time when problem student behaviors are most likely to occur, usually in the afternoon. Consistent observations and record keeping throughout the consultation will provide a continuous record of the severity of and changes in problem student behaviors. It is frequently desirable and more meaningful to the teacher to illustrate the data obtained from the observation records in the form of a graph (*see* the sample behavior graph).

While observing in the classroom, the consultant should have as little effect upon student behaviors as possible. The teacher, as a result of skills developed during the consultation, should be the primary influence on student classroom behaviors. The consultant *should not*, in any manner, interact with the students or teacher during the observation periods. The teacher should be instructed to tell the class before observations begin, "There will be a visitor coming into the classroom periodically. He will be doing some work in the back of the room, so please do not disturb him." Typically, students acclimate to the presence of the observer by the third observation period.

Baseline and Treatment

The measurement of student behaviors consists of two phases. In the first, the *baseline* phase, the target behaviors are observed and recorded during a series of observation periods prior to any efforts to change them. Baseline observations continue until a reliable index of the severity of these behaviors is established; in other words, the consultant should obtain a reasonably consistent sample of the occurrence of problem behaviors. Generally, the baseline phase consists of five to ten observations made during a two-week period. The second phase, the *treatment* phase, consists of observing and recording behaviors after efforts to remedy problem behaviors have begun. Treatment observations continue until the end of the consultation. Through a comparison of the frequency of problem behaviors during the treatment phase with their frequency during the baseline period, the effectiveness of the procedures can be determined. A decline in the severity of the problem behaviors indicates that the teacher's efforts have been productive.

Teacher Behaviors

Observations and recordings of the teacher's behavior are also desirable during the observation periods. Such observations will assist the consultant in assessing where changes in the teacher's interactions with students are needed. The teacher's strengths can also be identified and later used as examples of effective utilization of behavioral principles. The observation of the teacher's behavior should provide the consultant with both cues and reinforcers for establishing desirable teacher behaviors.

It may also be useful to have the teacher record his or her own interactions with students, noting the number of times he or she attends to desirable student behaviors or undesirable behaviors and provides instructions to the students (*see* example of the teacher interaction record). Teachers accustomed to using punitive methods for managing students may find it difficult to remember to look for and respond to good student behaviors. For these teachers, self-recordings serve as cues to remind them to interact more positively with their students.

Consultation Agenda

The majority of the responsibility for measuring behaviors through classroom observations falls on the consultant; however, the teacher should be exposed to and have an understanding of how and why these observations are made. The teacher should also understand why self-recordings of his or her own behaviors are useful. These understandings of the measurement of behaviors should result in an increase in the teacher's ability to objectively evaluate changes that occur both in student behaviors and in his or her own behavior. The following agenda is suggested for making classroom observations and developing the teacher's understanding of the measurement of behaviors.

AGENDA

1. *Develop an observation recording sheet prior to discussing the measurement of behaviors with the teacher.* Establish codes to be used for recording the operationally defined problem student behaviors during the classroom observations. List the names of students who will be observed in the order in which they will be observed. Specify the period during which each of these students will be observed. The number of these periods is reflected in the number of boxes after each student's name (*see* examples of the observation format and the observation sheet).
2. *Discuss the purpose for making classroom observations with the teacher.* Tell him or her that it provides a continuous and objective record of changes that take place in student behaviors. It also provides the basis for evaluating the effectiveness of treatment procedures.
3. *Explain to the teacher how the observations will be made.*

Demonstrate using a sample observation sheet.
4. *Have the teacher keep a record of the types of interactions he or she has with the student (see example of teacher interaction record).* This record will give the consultant an index of how the teacher typically interacts with the students and will make it necessary that the teacher develop a better awareness of his or her own behaviors. Establish a time when these records will be collected.
5. *Begin making baseline observations as soon as possible.* Data from each observation period can be illustrated graphically (*see* the sample behavior graph).

The primary question to be answered at this point of the consultation is "How is the severity of problem student behaviors and subsequent changes in these behaviors going to be measured?"

Observation Format

The following observation form is used to record the occurrence of specified problem student behaviors during baseline and treatment observations. The names of students are listed on the left side of the form. Each student is observed for approximately three seconds, which is sufficient to determine what the student is doing. If the student is on task behaving appropriately a slash mark (/) is recorded in the box to the right of the student's name. If the student is engaged in a problem behavior, the appropriate code representing the behavior is recorded. It is useful to distinguish between inappropriate and disruptive problem behaviors. Some codes for student behaviors might include the following:

/ = on task, desirable behaviors
0 = inappropriate but not disruptive (student at desk and quiet but daydreaming or sleeping)
S = out of seat
N = making noise
P = playing
F = fighting
T = throwing objects

After a recording is made, the observer proceeds on to the next student. After each student has been observed once, the observer goes to the top of the second column and observes and records the behavior of each student again. This cycle is repeated for each of the twenty columns on the observation form. An index of the severity of problem behaviors, for each observation period, can be obtained by counting the number of problem behaviors recorded, multiplying by five, and dividing by the number of students observed. The percentage of behaviors observed that were problematic can be calculated in this manner. These percentages can be plotted on a graph to illustrate changes in student behaviors that occur over observation periods. Similarly, percentages can be calculated for on task, inappropriate, or specific disruptive behaviors. Throughout the observation period, positive and negative teacher behaviors and *other information that will assist in developing procedures for correcting problem behaviors should be noted on the bottom of the observation form.*

OBSERVATION FORM

Teacher_____ Grade_____ Room_____ Observer_____
Subject_____ # of Students_____ Date_____ Time_____

Student Names	1	2	3	4	5	6	7	8	9	10	11	12	13	14	15	16	17	18	19	20

Comments:

CHANGES IN PROBLEM STUDENT BEHAVIORS
OVER OBSERVATION PERIODS

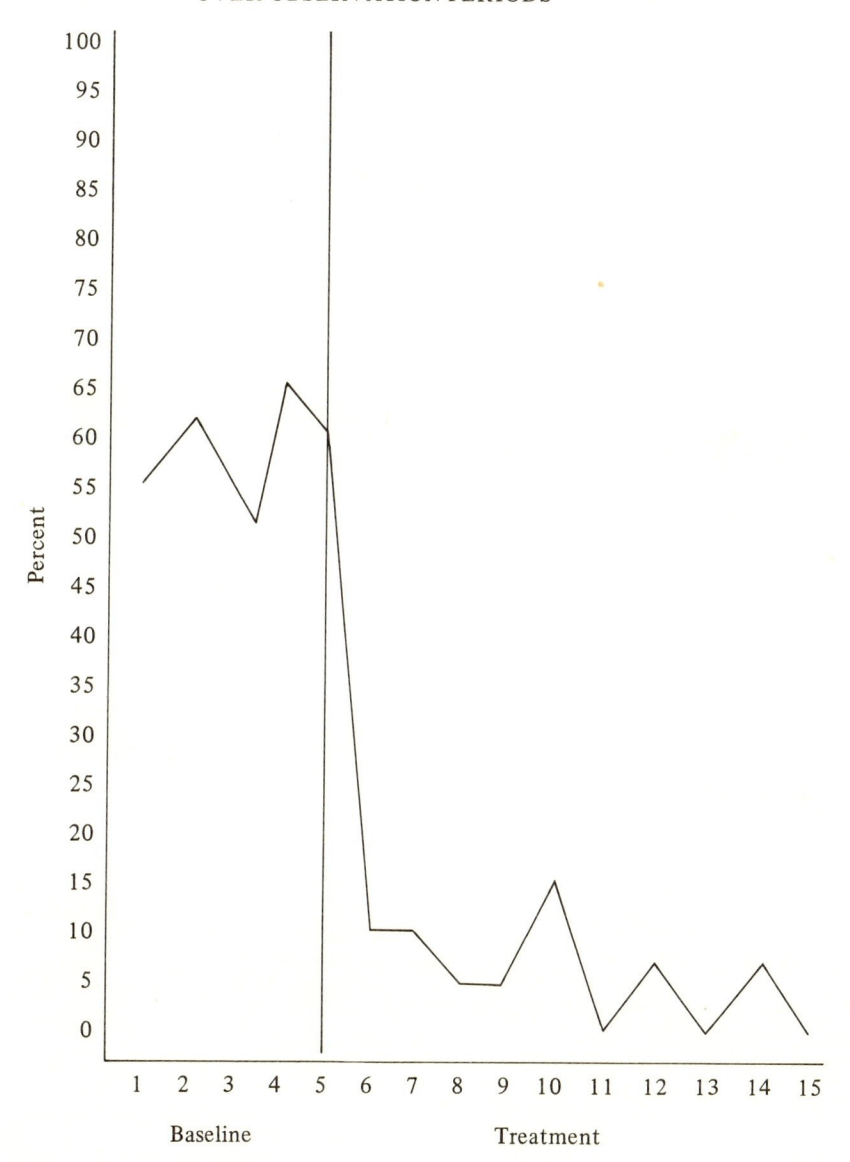

Classroom Management

TEACHER INTERACTION RECORD

Date:_____

Please record the praise (+) or punishment (-) that you provide to students by recording a + or - next to the appropriate time. Each response should be indicated by one mark.

8:00
9:00
10:00
11:00
12:00
1:00
2:00
3:00

Comments:

Reminders:

1. Look for good student behaviors to praise.
2. Praise efforts and improvements.
3. Vary your praise.
4. Praise loudly enough so that other students hear.
5. Use good students as models for others.
6. Don't praise the same student too frequently.
7. Make sure students know why they are praised.

Chapter 7

SPECIFYING DESIRABLE STUDENT BEHAVIORS

DESIRABLE student behaviors are those that the teacher desires and expects the students to engage in while at school. It is assumed that engaging in these behaviors will foster both the academic and social development of the students. In specifying desirable student behaviors, the same behavioral considerations apply when specifying problem student behaviors. The desirable behaviors should be specified in *observable* terms that describe *measurable behaviors* desired of the students. When these are clearly specified, the teacher can respond to and reinforce these desirable behaviors rather than focus solely on decreasing problem student behaviors. The function of the consultant at this point of the consultation is to assist the teacher in specifying desirable student behaviors, shifting the focus of discussion from problem student behaviors to the desirable ones that are to replace the problem behaviors. Here, the consultant should discuss the distinction between behavioral deficits and excesses, incompatible behaviors, long-term and short-term goals, shaping, and classroom rules.

Behavioral Deficits

For the purposes of this manual, desirable student behaviors are considered as behavioral deficits, behaviors the problem students should be engaged in but are not. Problem behaviors, in contrast, are considered as behavioral excesses (*see* Chapter 4). They are the behaviors the problem students are currently engaging in but should not be. To change student behaviors, both the problem and desirable student behaviors should be specified. However, it is important to maintain a clear distinction between problem behaviors and desirable behaviors. Desirable behaviors should not be specified in terms of what the student should not be doing. An example of inappropriately stating a desirable behavior would be "I (the teacher) would like the students to stop making so much noise and stop running around the room all the time." In this example, what the students should be doing is not specified. Problem behaviors, behavioral excesses of the students that the teacher wishes to stop, are specified. Specifying desirable behaviors, what the students should be doing instead of making noise and running around the room, would provide a direction of efforts to change student behaviors; for example, "I would like the students to work on their class assignments quietly at their desks" begins to identify a direction for change. Though "working on their assignments" could be further clarified, this example does identify student behavioral deficits, the desirable student behaviors that the teacher would like to increase. Examples of desirable student behaviors include staying seated at his or her desk, being quiet, raising hand for teacher assistance, working hard on class assignments, or following instructions.

Incompatible Behaviors

Student problems are described in terms of what a student *does*, but the implication is that the student should be doing something else. When a student is described as engaging in problem behaviors, the desirable behaviors that are to replace the problem behaviors should also be specified. Consider, for example, the student who "mopes around the room after finishing the assignment." Here it is easy to identify what the student *should not* be doing — moping around. However, what the student *should* be doing instead is not specified. If efforts to decrease the problem behavior are successful but a desirable behavior to replace the problem behavior has not been decided upon, the problem behavior that is decreased may be replaced by another problem behavior. No longer moping around, the student may now start daydreaming or sleeping. In order to reduce the possibility of one problem behavior being replaced by another, a desirable behavior *incompatible* with the occurrence of the problem behavior should be specified. Perhaps instead of "moping around" the student could be erasing the board. If this behavior was established, the student could not be "moping around"; erasing the board is a desirable behavior incompatible with "moping around," since both behaviors cannot occur at the same time. In changing problem student behaviors, the objective is not solely to decrease or eliminate problem behaviors but also to establish desirable behaviors that are incompatible with the occurrence of problem behaviors.

Long-term and Short-term Goals

When describing desirable student behaviors, the teacher may tend to use general categories of behaviors to express his or her expectations. For example, the teacher may say "I want them to be good students, to be courteous, and to behave properly." Though most teachers would readily agree that these are desirable student characteristics, there are two problems in using generalities such as these to set goals for student behaviors. The first has previously been discussed. In the example, the teacher's expectations do not describe specific measurable student behaviors. As a result, the students, teacher, and consultant may not be aware of the actual student behaviors that will satisfy the teacher's expectations. The second problem involves the distinction between long-term and short-term goals. Even after the teacher's expectations are specified in terms of observable student behaviors, these behaviors may be too numerous or too difficult for the student(s) to learn immediately. Thus, component behaviors that together comprise "being a good student" may each be viewed as a separate short-term goal. Teaching a student to be a "good student," the long-term goal, is a gradual process in which the establishment of each component behavior is a step towards that goal. Desirable student behaviors should be specified in terms of expected behaviors and these expected behaviors should be ones students can accomplish.

When discussing desirable student behaviors with the consultant, the teacher may confuse long-term and short-term goals. For example, a teacher may want the students to "sit in their seats and be quiet." The teacher, however, may also desire the students to "learn from each other in an open classroom setting." These desires indicate contradictory teacher expectations, a need to define the situations when one behavior is appropriate and the other not, or the difference between a long-term goal and one of the prerequisite steps involved in accomplishing it. "Learning from each other in an open classroom setting" may be a desirable long-term goal once it is clarified in terms of actual student behaviors. Achieving this goal, however, may mean that the student(s) has already learned or will learn certain prerequisite behaviors. These prerequisities might be student self-management skills, cooperative behaviors, or the ability to function at a specifiable level of academic proficiency. It is not realistic to expect a student who cannot work quietly at his or her seat to be able to function well in an open classroom setting. A distinction should be maintained between long-term goals and the prerequisite steps (short-term goals) that may need to be accomplished to arrive at the long-term goal.

Shaping

Desirable student behaviors are behaviors to be increased through cueing, positive reinforcement, and shaping. Shaping is the process of reinforcing gradual improvements in behavior. This is a very important principle for teachers to understand and utilize in their efforts to develop these behaviors. Even after the teacher's expectations are specified in terms of observable behaviors and long-term and short-term goals, all of the students may not want or immediately be able to meet the teacher's expectations. For example, it may be unreasonable to expect a student who has never done any math work and does not like math to abruptly change and do all his or her math work correctly. Here it would be desirable for the teacher to shape the student's behavior by reinforcing efforts the student might make to complete the math. Shaping might involve reinforcing the student for starting the math assignment one day, reinforcing him or her for doing two math problems correctly the next day, completing four problems the next day, and so on until the student is reinforced for completing all of the assigned math work. To get the student to do the math work (the goal) the teacher would gradually increase the criteria for his or her reinforcement, reinforcing successive improvements in the student's behavior.

Classroom Rules

There should be a clear and mutual understanding between the teacher and students of the desirable student behaviors the teacher expects from the students while in the classroom. Desirable student behaviors can be presented to the students as classroom rules or codes of conduct. Typical examples of general classroom rules include sitting in seat, being quiet, raising hand, and working hard. Classroom rules should be posted in the classroom to act as cues for student behaviors. Each desired behavior should be expressed in as few words as possible. The number of behaviors or rules should not be excessive; generally five or fewer is best. The posters of rules should be readable from across the classroom and should be placed in highly visible locations easy for both teacher and students to refer to. When explaining the classroom rules, the teacher should clarify them for the students by giving examples of when and how these behaviors are expected to occur and by having the students demonstrate how to follow and not follow the rules.

Consultation Agenda

The development of the teacher's skill in specifying desirable student behaviors should result in his or her ability to specify observable and measurable behaviors that are to be increased, thus replacing the problem student behaviors. Developing this skill includes providing the teacher with an understanding of the purposes for specifying incompatible desirable student behaviors to be increased. The development of this skill should result in a list of desired student behaviors that can be presented to the students as classroom rules. Following is an agenda and examples for this segment of the consultation.

AGENDA

1. *Provide a definition of "desirable student behaviors."* They are behaviors that the teacher expects and desires from the students. They are student behaviors to be increased.
2. *Discuss the guidelines for and utility of specifying desirable student behaviors.* The guidelines include specifying behavioral deficits, incompatible behaviors, long-term and short-term goals, shaping, and classroom rules. Desirable student behaviors are to replace problem behaviors. They provide a direction in which student behaviors should be changed.
3. *Identify the desirable student behaviors that the teacher would like to increase.* Ask for examples and clarifications when the teacher's expectations are not stated in terms of measurable student behaviors.
4. *Define the classroom rules, which will encompass the desired student behaviors.* The classroom rules are general statements of behaviors that students *should* engage in. However, the teacher should be prepared to further define these rules in terms of specific behaviors by giving students specific examples of the behaviors included under each rule. Classroom rules will be discussed again in Chapter 12.
5. *Have the teacher draw up two posters listing five or fewer classroom rules.* The posters will be posted in the classroom after procedures are developed to change student behaviors.

The primary question to be answered at this point of the consultation is "What should the students be doing?"

Chapter 8

IDENTIFYING POSITIVE REINFORCERS

POSITIVE reinforcers can be anything that a student wants and will engage in required behaviors to obtain. They can be something tangible, such as toys and candy, or they can be primarily social in nature, such as recognition and praise. Behaviors that are followed by a positive reinforcer are strengthened and tend to be repeated. Since the remediation of problem student behaviors concentrates on the replacement of these behaviors with desirable ones, positive reinforcers used to strengthen desirable behaviors must be identified. The classroom teacher, however, must be the one to provide positive reinforcers for desirable student behaviors. The function of the consultant at this point of the consultation is to assist the teacher in identifying reinforcing consequences that can be used to strengthen desirable student behaviors.

Intent versus Effect

A reinforcer is defined by its effect on behavior. A reinforcer increases the probability that the behavior that it immediately follows will occur again. If the behavior does not increase, the consequence of the behavior was not a reinforcer even though it was intended to be one. When identifying a reinforcer, the teacher must determine if it is currently viewed by the *student* as desirable and if the student will engage in the behaviors necessary to obtain the reinforcer. In other words, the selection of reinforcers should not be based solely on the assumptions of the consultant or teacher. They should not presume that an intended reinforcer will be effective for all students in a class since they will vary in age, sex, and ethnic, social, and economic backgrounds. It is the learning history of individual students that determines if or to what extent an intended reinforcer will be effective in strengthening a specified behavior.

Whether or not the consequence of a behavior is a positive reinforcer is based on an empirical assessment. If the occurrence of a specified student behavior increases following the presentation of an intended positive reinforcer, positive reinforcement has occurred. If it does not, then other consequences must be tried until effective positive reinforcers are identified.

Types of Reinforcers

When identifying reinforcers it is useful to divide positive reinforcers into three types — social, activity, and tangible. Social reinforcers — verbal praise, attention, physical gestures conveying approval or understanding (pats on the back, smiles, handshakes) — are the most important type of reinforcer and should always be used. They are essential to maintaining desirable student behaviors in a natural classroom setting. This kind of reinforcer is interactive by nature, involving both implicit and explicit communication between two or more individuals. Also, both the content and context of the communication are factors influencing the effectiveness of social reinforcers. The classroom teacher must be highly skilled in communicating and interacting with students in order to be socially reinforcing for them. For many teachers praising students may be awkward and seem superficial but, as with other skills, delivering social reinforcers becomes more natural for the teacher with practice. (Teacher-student interactions are discussed in greater detail in Chapter 10.)

Activities — playing games, participating in art projects, being class monitor, passing out paper, delivering messages, erasing boards, and having other special privileges — are generally desirable as reinforcers since they are readily available in and natural to classroom settings. They are especially useful as supplements to social reinforcers in maintaining desirable student behaviors. In highly disruptive classrooms, however, the use of activities as reinforcers may only contribute to the occurrence of disruptive behaviors. Thus, their use in *establishing* desirable behaviors in highly disruptive classrooms may not be feasible. In these classrooms, tangible reinforcers can be used instead. Once desired behaviors have been established, they can be maintained by activities and social reinforcers.

Tangible reinforcers — candy, snacks, trinkets, toys — are the most basic type of positive reinforcer and should be used in conjunction with social reinforcers when social reinforcers alone are not sufficient and the use of activities is not feasible. However, several problems may arise when tangible reinforcers are used. In addition to the possible teacher objection to their use, both the teacher and students may become dependent on them. The teacher may rely on them rather than develop the skills necessary to effectively provide social reinforcers. Some students may come to expect tangible reinforcers for everything they do; for others, the novelty of tangible reinforcers may wear out. When tangible reinforcers are used, plans should be developed to gradually remove and replace them with social and perhaps activity reinforcers once the desirable behaviors have been established.

The use of tangible reinforcers does have several definite assets. In highly disruptive classrooms, the reinforcers used to establish desirable behaviors will compete with the reinforcers currently maintaining the disruption. In this situation, the use of tangibles will enhance the value of the social reinforcers of desirable behaviors. Another possible advantage involves the *quick* establishment of these behaviors. Desirable changes in student behaviors are reinforcing to the teacher. If, however, these changes occur too slowly, the teacher's efforts may diminish. The use of tangible reinforcers usually facilitates quick changes. A third asset is the structure provided when tangible reinforcers are used. For a teacher unskilled in positive teacher-student interactions, using tangible reinforcers provides opportunities for that teacher to establish himself or herself as an effective social reinforcer by associating or pairing his or her interactions with the delivery of tangible reinforcers. Again, however, the consultant should remember that if tangible reinforcers are used, emphasis should always be placed on enhancing the effectiveness of the social reinforcers delivered by the teacher, reinforcers that will subsequently replace the tangible reinforcers and maintain the desirable student behaviors.

Enhancing the Effectiveness of Reinforcers

To enhance the effectiveness of tangibles and activities as reinforcers, the students should be allowed to participate in their selection. Student selections are, after all, more accurate indicators of effective positive reinforcers than are teacher or consultant selections. The problem with allowing this, however, is that a student may identify something that the teacher cannot or does not want to provide because it costs too much, parents or school officials may object, or it would cause classroom disturbances. Rejection of a student's suggestion could, quite obviously, result in disappointment and the student's unwillingness to accept alternative reinforcers. It is preferable to allow students to select tangibles and activities from alternatives that the teacher has already judged acceptable. Tangible items should be appropriate in price to the behavioral requirements that earn them. Generally, ten to twenty-five cent items are sufficient daily tangible reinforcers for students up to the fifth grade. Activities used as reinforcers should be natural to the classroom setting (extra library or gym time, movies, spelling bees, and special projects). Tangibles and activities that are used as reinforcers should not be available to the students while they are in school, except on a contingent basis. They should, however, be readily available to the teacher for immediate delivery to the students as they are earned.

There are four guidelines for the effective use of tangibles, activities, and social reinforcers. First, the students should be able to select from a variety of tangibles and activities — this will prevent satiation. In addition, the teacher should be able to provide a variety of social reinforcers. Second, there should be a clearly understood relationship between the student's behaviors and the reinforcers. When a student earns a reinforcer, he or she should be told what was done that earned it. Third, the temporal relationship between a student's behavior and a reinforcer is important. The reinforcer should always *follow* the desired student behavior, the delivery of the reinforcer occurring *immediately* after the student fulfills the criteria for reinforcement. Finally, the tone of the teacher's voice, facial expressions, the content and context of praise, the preconceptions of the students, and peer mores are some of the many factors that influence the effectiveness of social reinforcers. The classroom teacher must be aware of these and must establish himself or herself as a mediator of positive social reinforcers (*see* Chapter 10).

Punishment

Although the emphasis in improving problem student behaviors should be on the replacement of problem behaviors with incompatible desirable student behaviors through positive reinforcement, there are some problem behaviors that may need to be dealt with immediately. These include behaviors that may result in injury, involve destruction of property, or are in violation of school policies. For these, the time required to establish incompatible desirable student behaviors may not be available; they must be stopped immediately, possibly by the use of punishment. Punishment, of course, generally involves the presentation of an aversive consequence following a problem behavior. For example, a student who gets into a fight may receive a reprimand from the principal and be required to bring his or her parents to school. Punishment may also involve the loss of positive reinforcers; a student who is caught copying the class assignment from someone else's work may be kept in during recess and have his or her grade lowered. It should be emphasized to the teacher that physical abuse or excessive mental abuse of students is not a desirable form of punishment. When serious student problems occur, the teacher should refer to school policies to decide what appropriate actions should be taken.

The use of punishment should be minimized, since it has several undesirable side effects. First, the aversive qualities that punishment has for the students may generalize. When punishment is frequently used, the students in the class may come to dislike the teacher, the classroom, or even being in school. Students will then behave in ways resulting in their avoidance of or escape from the punishing classroom situations. Second, the teacher who uses excessive punishment may become an aversive stimulus to the students, making it difficult for the teacher to socially reinforce desirable student behaviors. Third, students will adapt to frequently used punishers, requiring the teacher to increase the intensity of the punishers in order to maintain their effectiveness. This escalation, in turn, may result in a classroom atmosphere generally aversive for both students and teacher.

As they are with desirable student behaviors, students should be made explicitly aware of the severe problem behaviors not tolerated in the classroom and of the consequences for engaging in these behaviors. In developing a classroom management program, a list of intolerable student behaviors can be posted as behaviors that will be punished. When a student engages in these disruptive behaviors, the student will then be punished. Punishment may involve the use of fines in which a student loses points he or she had earned or may involve timeout in which a student is removed from the classroom for a specified period of time. (Procedures for addressing problem student behaviors are suggested in Chapter 11.)

Consultation Agenda

The development of the teacher's skill in identifying reinforcers for student behaviors should result in his or her ability to list the reinforcing consequences that strengthen desirable student behaviors. Developing this teacher skill includes providing the teacher with an understanding of the guidelines for identifying effective reinforcers and enhancing their effectiveness.

AGENDA

1. *Provide the teacher with a definition of "positive reinforcer."* Positive reinforcers can be anything that a student wants and will engage in required behaviors to obtain.
2. *Discuss the guidelines for identifying effective reinforcers.* These include intent versus effect and the types of rein-

forcers. Explain the usefulness of each type of reinforcer. Decide the types of reinforcers that will be used.
3. *Discuss ways of enhancing the effectiveness of reinforcers.* This includes student participation in their selection, magnitude, variety, availability, immediacy, content, and context.
4. *List possible reinforcers by type.* Make a tentative list of reinforcers that the teacher can use to discuss with the students and subsequently revise (*see* example of list of reinforcers).
5. *Discuss and identify possible punishers.* This includes response cost, time-out, and school policies (*see* the example of a time out slip).

The primary question that should be answered at this point in the consultation is "What reinforcers will be used to strengthen desirable student behaviors?"

Reinforcers

SOCIAL	ACTIVITIES	TANGIBLE
Verbal:	movies	candy
Right	passing out papers	toys
Good	messenger	snacks
Excellent	art projects	cookies
Perfect	games	pickles
Fine	stories	apples
O.K.	spelling bees	art and hobby supplies
That's smart	gym	jewelry
You're doing	library	books
fine.	erasing boards	school material
I like the way . . .		
You must be		
proud of . . .		

Gestures:
  smile
  wink
  handshake
  pat on the back

TIME-OUT SLIP

This student has been sent from the classroom because of his/her disruptive behavior. Please have this student remain in time-out for 15 minutes. While in time-out <u>this student should sit quietly</u> facing a wall. He/She should <u>not</u> be allowed to talk with anyone, play, run errands, etc. Please indicate the time he/she arrived and the time he/she left time-out and sign the slip below.

STUDENT NAME:_____ DATE:_____

TIME LEFT CLASSROOM:_____ TEACHER:_____

TIME ARRIVED TIME-OUT:_____ TIME-OUT SUPERVISOR:_____

TIME LEFT TIME-OUT:_____ _____

TIME RETURNED TO CLASSROOM:_____

COMMENTS:

Chapter 9

SPECIFYING CONTINGENT RELATIONSHIPS

CONTINGENCIES are the dependent relationships between specified behaviors and their consequences. In order to change a behavior, the contingent relationship between that behavior and its consequence must be restructured. Desirable student behaviors are strengthened by providing reinforcing consequences. Undesirable student behaviors are weakened by removing reinforcing consequences and, perhaps, by punishing the student for those behaviors. Specifying contingencies involves stating the dependent relationship between the behavior to be strengthened or weakened and the consequence that will be provided in order to promote the desired behavior change. In the classroom, it is the teacher who is responsible for specifying student behaviors and for providing appropriate consequences. The function of the consultant at this point of the consultation is to assist the teacher in removing reinforcing consequences for identified problem student behaviors and in structuring the identified reinforcers in a manner that will strengthen the specified desirable student behaviors.

If — Then

Contingencies indicate causal relationships. *If* a student does this, *then* this will happen. *If* refers to the occurrence of an observably specified student behavior — the behavioral criterion. *Then* refers to the specified reinforcer or punisher that will directly follow the behavior. Teachers frequently express their expectations to the students through such commands as "sit down, be quiet, and get to work." The intent of this type of statements is to convey to the students the behaviors that the teacher desires. The consequences for student behaviors, however, are often overlooked by the teacher. As a result, these statements frequently have little functional meaning for the students. Though the students may understand the meaning of the words used to express desired behaviors, these words have little effect on the behaviors of the students because the consequences for either engaging or not engaging in the desired behaviors have not been specified. In order for the teacher's statements to have a functional meaning, the contingent relationship between the desired student behavior and its consequences must be specified.

The effectiveness of a contingency is determined by the resulting change in student behaviors. To foster positive changes in student behaviors, the emphasis should be on *replacing* problem behaviors by providing reinforcing consequences for desirable student behaviors. If the desired change in student behavior does not occur, the contingent relationship between the behavior and its consequence should be reexamined with the following guidelines in mind: The desired behavior and its consequence should *immediately follow* the behavior. There should be numerous explicit cues for the students indicating the desired behaviors. Severe problem behaviors that are not tolerable should also be clearly understood by the students. The contingent relationship between the students' behaviors and their consequences should be clearly stated to the students.

Mutually Acceptable

Contingent relationships should be mutually acceptable to, as well as understood by, both teacher and students. The student behaviors that will fulfill the behavioral criteria for reinforcement should be described in detail. The behavioral criteria should include the description of an observable student behavior, the frequency of the expected behavior, and the time limitations and other conditions within which the behavior is to occur. When activities or tangible reinforcers are to be used, they should also be described in detail. The magnitude of the reinforcer, when it will be made available, and the procedures for obtaining the reinforcers should be specified. All of these conditions must be mutually acceptable to the teacher and students if the student management program is to be successful.

Two procedures are useful to ensure that the teacher and students have a mutually acceptable understanding of these contingent relationships. These are *modeling* and *role-playing*. *Modeling* is a demonstration by the teacher of the desired student behaviors. The teacher behaves in ways that will meet the behavioral criteria. *Role-playing* involves some students taking the role of students who are fulfilling the behavioral criteria and others the role of students who are not. The students can be asked questions such as "Which students are behaving properly? What are they doing? What will happen because of their good behaviors? Which students are not behaving properly?" Modeling and role-playing are also useful for practice and clarification during consultation sessions between consultant and teacher.

Shaping is a third device for specifying contingencies. Normally, the behavior expected of the student should be within the student's immediate performance ability. If, however, the desired change in the student's behavior is difficult for the student to fulfill, the student's behavior should be shaped. *Shaping* involves the breaking down of a difficult or complex behavior into a series of small steps. Each step the student completes is then reinforced. Thus, in shaping a behavior, the gradual improvement a student makes toward fulfilling the desired but difficult behavior is reinforced, sequentially fostering the student's learning progress. Care must be taken to see that the desired behavior specified in a contingency is not highly complex or too difficult. Care must also be taken to provide a reinforcer that is comparable in magnitude to the difficulty of the desired behavior.

Feedback

An effective contingency should provide for periodic feedback from the teacher to the student concerning the progress made by the student towards fulfilling the behavioral criteria. Providing this periodic information allows the teacher to cue student behaviors and reinforce student progress and provides opportunities for students to correct their behaviors. The teacher should circulate frequently through the classroom to assist the students in both their academic and social behaviors. To ensure that feedback is not overlooked, specific times for feedback should be scheduled throughout the day.

Feedback is primarily verbal and has three components that should be considered by the teacher in giving verbal feedback — statement, praise, and expectation. In the *statement,* the student should be told what he or she has done, for example, "You've sat quietly working on your math all morning." When the student's behavior is desirable or is an improvement, the statement should be followed by *praise,* for example, "I'm very proud of you." However, when the student's behavior is not desirable and is not an improvement, this component — praise — should obviously be omitted. In the last component, *expectation,* the teacher should cue the student for future behaviors, for example, "Keep up the good work." Expectations are especially important when the student's behavior is not completely satisfactory. "You've done three of the math problems. I would like you to finish the rest by ten o'clock." After expectations have been stated by the teacher, he or she should follow through by checking to see whether the student has met them. If the student has, teacher praise should then be given. Whenever possible, feedback should emphasize what the student has done right and should be summarized by social reinforcers.

When tangible reinforcers are used as part of the initial management procedure, they should *not* be emphasized by the teacher during the feedback. The students should already have a clear understanding of what the reinforcers are. To overemphasize them could result in desirable student behaviors becoming too dependent on them. Such dependency may make it difficult to establish effective social reinforcers. Furthermore, this overemphasis may also be misperceived by the student as a threat. The student may then reject both the feedback and the reinforcers.

Consistency

Consistency is the most important factor determining the effectiveness of a contingency. There must be consistency between what is specified in the contingency and what actually happens. If a student engages in the desired behaviors and meets the behavioral critieria, the teacher must provide the specified reinforcer. For example, a behavioral criterion might be that the student is supposed to complete twenty math problems correctly by recess. The reinforcer might be five minutes of extra recess. If the student correctly completes twenty math problems ten minutes before recess, the student has fulfilled the behavioral criterion and should be allowed the extra recess time. Though the teacher may subsequently believe that the student could have done five more math problems, the teacher must still deliver the reinforcer in order to maintain his or her credibility with the student. The teacher could, however, reassess the behavioral criterion and change it accordingly *next time*. Students learn to engage or not engage in behaviors that are *consistently* associated with reinforcing or punishing consequences. Inconsistency in contingencies results in inconsistent student behaviors. As part of a consistent program, desirable student behaviors and their consequences should be periodically reviewed with the students to avoid misunderstandings. The students must continually be aware that specified consequences consistently follow specified behaviors.

Individual and Group Contingencies

Contingencies can be established to change not only the behaviors of an individual student but also of a group of students or a whole class. If the target for change is an individual student, contingencies can be considered as an individual contingency contract, an agreement between the teacher and the student. Here the consultant generally acts as a mediator between the teacher and student, drawing up a contingency contract acceptable to both the teacher and the student. The contract specifies the desired student behaviors, a format for recording the occurrence of the desired behavior, the criteria for reinforcement, and the reinforcer. Unfortunately, a major problem in setting up such contingencies for an individual student in the classroom is that other students may perceive the agreement as unfair to them. The problem student can earn a specified reinforcer while others cannot. If it arises, this problem may be alleviated by involving the parents and asking them to provide reinforcers at home for reports of good classroom behaviors.

When several students are the targets for change, it may be preferable to establish a contingency program — a classroom management program — involving the entire class. Generally, this is desirable when there are five or more problem students and the desired behaviors are similar for all the students in question. As previously mentioned, setting up a classroom management program involves the specification of desirable student behaviors by writing classroom rules to be posted in the classroom, developing a teacher record system to monitor student behaviors, identifying the types of reinforcers that can be earned by the students, establishing behavioral criteria for reinforcement, and establishing procedures for addressing intolerable problem student behaviors.

The behavioral criteria for reinforcement in such a program should be specified so that each student earns a reinforcer at his or her own pace. One criterion for reinforcement might be that a student must complete five pages in the math workbook. One student may meet the criteria in one hour; it may take another student three hours. Time restrictions can, however, be part of the criterion; for example, a student must complete five pages in the math workbook by 10 AM. Some students may not meet the behavioral criterion within the allotted time. A behavioral criterion should be set so that approximately 80 percent of the students should be able to meet it. If it is not, the contingencies may lose their effectiveness.

The behavioral criterion for reinforcement can also be given on a group contingency basis; that is, the reinforcer will be available only if all the students in an assigned group meet that criterion. A group may consist of rows or columns of students or the total class; for example, "If the row you sit in is quiet all morning, then all the students in that row will have an extra five minutes of recess." One student in a group can then prevent the group from earning the reinforcer. Group contingencies generally increase peer pressure, further fostering the desired changes in each student in the group. However, group contingencies also increase the possibility of resentment of and retaliation against students who hold the group back. Such feelings can be forestalled somewhat by periodically changing the members of each group.

Regardless of the manner in which the contingencies are set up, individual differences and shaping should be allowed for. The teacher should continually provide social reinforcers for student efforts and improvements even though these may not be specified in an explicit contingent relationship. Ideally, the behaviorally skilled teacher will utilize contingency management and shaping principles at all times, both explicitly and implicitly in interacting with the students in the classroom.

Explicit and Implicit Contingencies

Contingencies are always influencing a person's behavior. Sometimes the contingent relationship between a person's behavior and its consequence is deliberately planned and sometimes it is not. Contingencies may be very apparent or very subtle in nature. They may involve an explicit statement of the relationship between a behavior and its consequence or they may only imply a relationship. To change student behaviors, both kinds of contingencies must be restructured.

A point system is an example of explicit contingencies. With a point system, students earn points by engaging in desired student behaviors (obeying classroom rules). The teacher monitors each student behavior by recording it in the teacher record. Periodically during each classroom day, the teacher assesses each student's behaviors, recording the number of points every student has earned on that student's point slip. At the end of the day, students who have earned a specified number of points (the criteria) can exchange their point slips for a reinforcer. In a point system, the relationship between the desired student behaviors and the reinforcers is clearly stated.

There are, however, many desirable student behaviors that may not be covered by classroom rules or by other explicit statements of desirable student behaviors. Examples of these might include continuing to do classwork even though there is an interruption by a visitor, returning lost items, volunteering for various tasks, and smiling and showing enthusiasm while working. These behaviors should be reinforced even though explicit contingencies have not been established. The teacher can provide recognition, praise, and other social reinforcers that imply that those behaviors are desirable. Teacher-student interactions provide continuous implicit cues and consequences — implicit contingencies — for student behaviors. It is essential in this regard that the teacher be able to assess the effects of his or her interactions on student behaviors and make corrections when appropriate. Because of its importance, developing positive teacher-student interactions will be covered in greater detail in Chapter 10.

Consultation Agenda

The development of a teacher's skills in specifying contingent relationships should result in his or her ability to structure the relationship between the specified student behaviors and consequences in a manner promoting desired changes in student behaviors. To develop this teacher's skill, the consultant should first provide the teacher with an understanding of the relationship among the topics covered in this section. Next, the principles of specifying contingencies should be reviewed.

AGENDA

1. *Provide the teacher with a definition of a "contingency."* Contingencies are statements of the dependent relationship between specified behaviors and their consequences.
2. *Discuss the principles involved in specifying contingencies.* *If-then* relationships, mutually acceptable, feedback, consistency, and individual versus group contingencies.

Specifying Contingent Relationships

3. *Develop procedures for strengthening desirable behaviors.**
   These include the use of posters of classroom rules, a point system, contingency contracts, and the delivery of reinforcers.
4. *Specify procedures for weakening problem behaviors.**
   These include ignoring, warning, fining, time-out, and school policies.
5. *Develop feedback procedures.** These may include the use of a point system and establishing time intervals for feedback.
6. *Rehearse and role-play the above procedures.* Practice reviewing classroom rules with students, giving points and verbal feedback, reinforcing desirable behaviors, punishing undesirable behaviors, and delivering tangible reinforcers.

The primary question to be answered at this point of the consultation is "How are the relationships between student behaviors and their consequences to be structured in order to establish the desired changes in those behaviors?"

---

*The classroom management program presented in Chapter 11 provides examples that should help to clarify these topics.

Chapter 10

DEVELOPING POSITIVE TEACHER-STUDENT INTERACTIONS

IN the classroom, the teacher is the mediator for a majority of the cues and consequences for student behaviors. Throughout the consultation, the teacher and consultant have worked to develop the teacher's skills in managing student behaviors in the classroom — to make the teacher a more effective mediator. Emphasis has been placed on increasing the teacher's positive value to the students so that he or she can effectively cue and provide consequences for student behaviors. Previous sections of this manual have presented many of these cues and consequences and examined how they can be structured to promote desired changes in student behaviors. Explicit cues — the posting of classroom rules, the writing of lessons on the board, verbal instructions to students — have the deliberate intent of specifying desirable student behaviors. Similarly, explicit consequences — gold stars, grades, or awards — dispensed by the teacher deliberately intend to reinforce desirable student behaviors. Cues and consequences are often implicit as well as explicit. What the teacher attends to and how the teacher attends to student behaviors provide cues and consequences quite apart from any deliberate intent to provide them. The teacher's behavior frequently provides models for the students to emulate. These implicit cues and consequences vary with the situations in which student-teacher interactions occur. The consultant should develop the teacher's awareness of the various effects that these interactions have on student behaviors and, when appropriate, provide the teacher with positive alternatives for interaction.

Guidelines for Teacher-Student Interactions

It is not possible to list all of the interactions that can and do occur between a teacher and student. Rather than attempting to do so, general guidelines are presented to help the teacher engage in positive teacher-student interactions and avoid confrontations or negative interactions.

1. *Each student starts out fresh everyday.* Previous problem behaviors should have been dealt with when they occurred. Reminding a student that you are angry with him for yesterday's behavior may only cause him to act up today. Consider the example of a teacher who says to a student, "Remember what happened yesterday? If it happens again, you'll be in the principal's office and your mother will be called." It is probable that a confrontation will occur given this situation. The student may resent the teacher's criticism and angrily reply, "So what! Go ahead and call her."

2. *Pay attention to students who are on task and behaving appropriately by frequently interacting with them, providing them with recognition and praise for their good behaviors.* More time should be spent with students who are engaged in desirable behaviors than with students who are disruptive. The teacher's attention is often an effective reinforcer for maintaining student behaviors. However, a teacher should not wait until a student becomes disruptive before he or she attends to that student. When praise is used, it should be sincere, enthusiastic, and loud enough for nearby students to hear.

3. *Ignore, whenever possible, students who are off task or not behaving appropriately.* Students who are not behaving properly should not be verbally abused by excessive criticism or by referring to them as class clowns, nuts, stupid, etc. Rather they should be cued to the proper behaviors. The teacher can say something like "Let's see who is working quietly." The teacher can then proceed to recognize those students. If the misbehaving student begins to work quietly, the teacher can then recognize him; for example, "Ann is working quietly, so is Bill, James, Joan, and I see that Larry has also started his work." When ig-

noring and cueing does not work and the student's problem behavior cannot be tolerated, the teacher should objectively tell the student what is expected of him and the consequences if he does not do it: "Larry, return to your seat and finish your classwork or you'll have to stay in during recess." Reprimands should be given in a soft voice, audible to only the misbehaving student.

4. *Be consistent in carrying out promises or threats made to students.* The teacher should not make promises or threats that he or she cannot or does not intend to carry out. Out of frustration, a teacher may say, "I'm going to send you all to reform school." Teacher statements such as this must lack credibility since the students know that they will not be carried out.

5. *Students should be told what behaviors are expected of them.* Classroom rules should be established and the students told that their behaviors, which they are responsible for, will determine the reinforcers or punishers that result. The teacher does not give reinforcers or punishers to the students; the students earn them by their classroom behaviors. The teacher should not ask students questions about their behavior that the teacher already knows the answer to, for example, "Did I tell you to scream and shout?" Again they should be told the behaviors that are expected of them.

6. *Give the students explicit instructions on class assignments.* These instructions should be reviewed so that there is no need for individual students to ask procedural questions about what they are to do. The teacher should periodically circulate through the class to assist students on these assignments. The teacher should not assume that the students know what to do and how to do it.

7. *Have something for the students to do at all times.* The teacher should have lessons prepared so that all class assignments can be started immediately, preventing the students from being distracted. Lessons that need to be written on the chalkboard should be placed there in advance. Supplementary material or activities should be made available for students who finish their assignments early. The teacher

should provide recognition for extra work done by students.
8. *The teacher should call on or respond only to those students who raise their hands.* Other means of getting the teacher's attention can be disruptive. Similarly, students should not be allowed at the teacher's desk without permission.
9. *Use other students as examples of good behavior.* Using a student's behavior as an example for others provides both recognition for the student and cues for other students. However, the same student should not be continually used as the example. It is preferable to use a student who does not usually receive recognition for the good behavior being noted.
10. *Make class work as enjoyable as possible.* Use learning games, spelling bees, stories, etc. to enhance the lessons. Individualize assignments and evaluate each student's work individually as much as possible so that each student will experience some degree of success. When correcting student work, mark the ones that are correct rather than the ones that are wrong. Do not use or threaten to use academic subjects as punishment for bad conduct.
11. *Send notes home to parents citing improvements in the student's academic and social behaviors.* Desirable student behaviors should be brought to the parents' attention. Parents are accustomed to receiving notes only for bad reports. Providing parents with good reports about their child's behavior at school could result in the child being encouraged and reinforced for these behaviors at home.
12. *Be objective when addressing problem student behaviors.* The student should be told what the problem behavior was and reminded that he or she is responsible for his or her behavior and its consequences. Long arguments and emotional confrontations with students concerning what they did or did not do should be avoided. The teacher should maintain a pleasant tone of voice and should not become angry with the student. The teacher should concentrate on clearly stating the behaviors expected from the student.

13. *Praise the entire class periodically when the class, in general, is quiet.* It is often tempting for the teacher to use these times to grade papers or catch up with his or her records. However, the teacher should remember to reinforce good classroom behaviors. For example, the teacher can say, "This is the quietest class in the school." "Everyone is really working hard. I'm proud of all of you." "This class will be complimented again by the principal for its good conduct."

The teacher must establish himself or herself as a mediator of positive social reinforcers. The students should come to associate the teacher with pleasant events, not with aversive ones. Positive teacher-student interactions will foster the development of positive student self-concepts and self-management of behaviors.

Problem Teacher Behaviors

During the classroom observations, part of the consultant's responsibility is to identify characteristic teacher behaviors that may be contributing to the occurrence of undesirable student behaviors. Below are some of these behaviors that may be observed in the classroom.

1. *The teacher may be inconsistent in the way he or she handles similar behaviors by different students.* The teacher's perception of a student often influences how the teacher interprets and responds to the student's behavior. A teacher may be more critical of the behavior of a student he or she perceives as a "troublemaker" than of the behavior of a student perceived as "creative." Such bias may cause a student to feel picked on and the teacher may eventually be seen as unfair.
2. *The teacher may not follow through in checking whether a student has done what he or she was asked to do.* The teacher's statements of expectations lose their "functional" meaning if they are not followed through. For example, the teacher may say to a student, "Sit down and finish your

work, and then I'll come over and check it." If the teacher does not subsequently check the student's work, the student may not bother to do future work.
3. *The teacher controls the class through the frequent use of punishment, threats, and intimidation.* The teacher becomes an aversive stimulus to the students and, therefore, is an ineffective positive reinforcer for desirable student behaviors. Student dislike of the teacher could result in student retaliation and other behaviors upsetting to the teacher.
4. *The teacher does not provide adequate reinforcers for desirable student behaviors.* Reinforcers may be inadequate for several reasons — the teacher's praise may lack warmth or enthusiasm; the praise may be too repetitive, e.g. "I like the way you do this." "I like the way you do that." "I like the way . . ."; tangible reinforcers made available contingently may also be available to the students noncontingently; the reinforcer's magnitude may not be sufficient for the behaviors required to earn it; etc.
5. *The teacher has not adequately prepared or organized the day's lessons.* There may be pauses after each lesson while the teacher prepares the next lesson. The teacher may not provide adequate instructions or the materials that are necessary to complete the assignment, the assignment is too difficult or boring for some students, or the students do not understand what they are to learn. All of these could contribute to the occurrence of problem student behaviors.

Consultation Agenda

Developing the teacher's awareness of how interactions with students affects student behaviors should result in an increase in positive teacher-student interactions.

AGENDA

1. *Discuss the importance of developing positive teacher-student interactions.* The teacher is a mediator for a majority of cues and consequences for student behaviors in the class-

room. The teacher's own behaviors affect student behaviors. The teacher must then establish positive teacher-student interactions in order to maintain desirable student behaviors.
2. *Review the guidelines for teacher-student interactions with the teacher.* Use examples based on the consultant's classroom observations to clarify these guidelines when possible.
3. *Provide the teacher with information based on the consultant's classroom observation and the teacher interaction record about his or her interactions.* During the classroom observations, the consultant should have noted both the positive and negative interactions that the teacher has had with students. It is important that the consultant stress the positive teacher-student interactions that have occurred. These provide recognition for desirable teacher behaviors and can be used later as examples for improving less desirable teacher-student interactions.
4. *Rehearse and role-play positive teacher-student interactions simulating situations likely to occur in the classroom.* These situations include what the teacher does when the students first come into the classroom, teacher feedback to students, ignoring and cueing student behaviors, socially reinforcing desirable student behaviors, and addressing problem student behaviors.

The primary question to be answered at this point of the consultation is "What should the teacher do to establish positive teacher-student interactions."

Chapter 11

A CLASSROOM MANAGEMENT PROGRAM

THE development of any classroom management program is based on information the consultant gathers as he or she proceeds through the problem solving steps presented in Chapters 4 through 10. The successful implementation of this program depends, in turn, on the teacher's skills developed as a result of the information provided to him or her during the problem solving process. After proceeding successfully through the problem solving process, the consultant, working with the teacher, is ready to integrate this information into a classroom management program implemented by the skilled teacher.

In the development and implementation of this program, there are several sequential goals for changing student behavior that both consultant and teacher should continuously be considering. These goals include establishing desirable student behaviors, establishing the teacher as a positive reinforcer, developing student self-management skills, and maintaining desirable student behaviors in a natural classroom setting. These goals are not mutually exclusive; rather, they substantially overlap. The emphasis on accomplishing a goal gradually shifts to the next goal as each is achieved. The procedures involved in a classroom management program also change gradually as each of the sequential goals are met. These procedural changes are reflected in the various "phases" of the classroom management program.

A classroom management program is presented here as an example of how the information gathered during the problem solving process is used to accomplish the goals for changing student behavior. The reader should understand that this problem solving process can be applied to the problem behaviors of a single student and need not lead to a program involving the entire class. Although the program that follows is designed for groups of students, the procedures presented here can be adapted to consultations that do not focus on an entire classroom.

This classroom management program has been effectively used in highly disruptive first through fifth grades, social adjustment classrooms, and special education classrooms. With modifications in the point system and types of reinforcers, this program has also been used effectively in sixth and seventh grade classrooms. The number of students in the classrooms varied from twelve to thirty-four, with most of the classrooms having thirty students and one teacher. The program was designed to quickly increase the occurrence of desirable student behaviors through the use of tangible reinforcers and then to maintain those desirable behaviors with social reinforcers and positive teacher-student interactions after the removal of tangible reinforcers and the point system. The management program has three basic procedural aspects: classroom observations, point system, teacher-student interactions.

Classroom Observations

Classroom observations were made three days per week — Monday, Wednesday, and Friday — from 1 to 2 PM. During these periods, recordings were made of student and teacher behaviors on the observation sheet. The format of these recordings is described in Chapter 6. Additional notes were also made to supplement the information provided to the teacher. These observations began two weeks prior to the implementation of the management program and continued through the consultation. Additional classroom observations were made when problem situations, as noted by the teacher, did not arise during scheduled observations.

Within the context of a management program, observations serve the following essential functions:

1. Observations provide a means to assess the degree of disruption occurring in the classroom and the factors that contribute to the disruption.
2. They provide a means to monitor and objectively evaluate

the effects of the management program upon the behaviors of the students.
3. They provide the basis for information to the teacher concerning desirable and undesirable teacher behaviors and their effects on student behaviors.

Point System

Each student earned points by behaving in manners specified by the classroom rules. Using the teacher record form, the teacher kept a record of each student's behavior during each of the specified intervals of time referred to as "point periods." An example of the teacher record follows at the end of this section. When recording student behaviors, the teacher should individualize his or her expectations of each student's ability to follow each of the classroom rules. The teacher should be sensitive to gradual improvements in student behaviors. A student should not be evaluated by comparison with other students but on the basis of the improvement made in his or her own behavior. Based on the data on the teacher record, the teacher assessed whether the student had earned a point for following each of the classroom rules during the specified point period. A point slip was given to each student at the beginning of each day. At the end of each specified point period, a point was recorded on the point slip for each of the classroom rules that the student had followed. Student behaviors during one point period should not affect the points a student can earn during subsequent point periods. While recording points on the student's point slip, the teacher also provided verbal feedback and praise, emphasizing the student's *good behaviors,* not the number of points earned. When a student did not earn a point, the teacher told the student what was expected of him or her. A zero should not be recorded on the student's point slip; when a student does not earn a point, the slip should be left blank. (An example of a point slip follows this chapter.) The number of points a student had earned during each point period was totalled at the end of each day. If the student had earned a specified number of points or more, the student exchanged his or her point slip for an award.

The major elements in the point system are the classroom rules, the phases in which the desirable student behaviors are established and those in which the tangible reinforcers and point system are phased out, and the procedures for addressing exceptionally good or excessively disruptive student behaviors.

CLASSROOM RULES: As a result of discussions with the teacher and classroom observations, the following five rules were established. These rules, which specified *desirable* student behaviors, were printed in large letters and posted in the classroom.

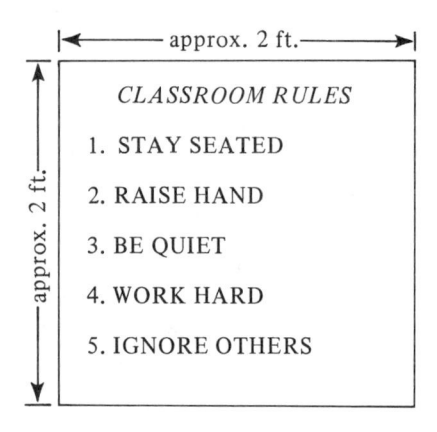

|← approx. 2 ft. →|

CLASSROOM RULES

1. STAY SEATED
2. RAISE HAND
3. BE QUIET
4. WORK HARD
5. IGNORE OTHERS

(approx. 2 ft.)

1. *Stay seated* meant that each student should be seated at his or her assigned desk and should be facing front unless otherwise instructed.
2. *Raise hand* meant that students should always raise their hands when seeking the attention of the teacher. Students should not attempt to gain the teacher's attention by shouting or grabbing the teacher.
3. *Be quiet* included unauthorized verbalizations and noises, such as whistling, humming, tapping feet, tapping pencils on desks, and slamming books, which might disturb other students.
4. *Work hard* meant that the students should be engaged in class assignments as indicated by behaviors such as reading, attending to the teacher during oral lessons, writing, etc.

5. *Ignore others* meant that each student was responsible for his or her own behavior. Students should continue to work on class assignments ignoring other students who caused disruptions.

PHASES: There were five phases during which changes in the reinforcers or point system occurred. These phases were discussed in general with the teacher. However, specific information concerning each phase was not provided to the teacher until the phase was to be implemented. This was done to avoid confusion and prevent the teacher from making premature changes in the program. At the beginning of each phase, the teacher was given a written summary outlining the procedures involved in that phase. These are presented at the end of this section.

Phase 1: On the day before the point system was to be implemented, the teacher was given a checklist of tasks that should be accomplished on that day. (*See* "The Day Before The Program Begins" following this chapter.) The first phase of the point system began the following morning. The teacher was provided with a daily checklist of teacher activities involved in that phase and an outline to use to explain the point system to the students. (*See* "Introducing the Program" at the end of this chapter.) The teacher's clear explanation of the program to the students, as well as the teacher's consistency in carrying out the program procedures, is extremely important. The consultant should observe in the classroom and be available to provide feedback and correct any procedural omissions or mistakes during the first day of the program. Point slips were passed out to the students. The teacher began *each* day by explaining the **point system and classroom rules.** During Phase 1, there were four point periods — the first from the beginning of class to the morning recess, the second from the morning recess to lunch, the third from lunch to the afternoon recess, and the fourth from the afternoon recess to dismissal. The teacher would begin recording points on student point slips and providing concise feedback to each student ten minutes before the end of each point period. Point periods typically ended at 10:30, 12:00, 2:00, and 3:00.

During each point period, the teacher recorded the occurrence of problem student behaviors on the teacher record. This record was then used to determine the number of points each student earned at the end of that point period. By following the five classroom rules, a student could earn 5 points during each point period or, since there were 4 point periods, a total of 20 points by the end of the classroom day. There were also bonus points and fines that affected the total number of points earned. Bonus points and fines are explained later. A student needed 16 points to be eligible for an award. The teacher's expectations of the students or the criteria for earning an award may be set too high if less than two-thirds of the students earn awards each day.

At the end of each day, the teacher, using the teacher record, called students individually to come up and select their awards. Students would be called in descending order of total points earned. Students earning the most points had the best selection among the awards for that day. The awards consisted of a variety of candy, toys, trinkets, and a few school supplies costing an average of twenty cents. Students would be congratulated by the teacher as they came up to select their awards. Generally, student behaviors improved dramatically during the first few days of Phase 1. Phase 1 continued for approximately two weeks. For at least one week before proceeding to Phase 2, the occurrence of undesirable student behaviors, as reflected in the data collected during the daily classroom observations, should have fallen to and remained below 5 percent of the total number of behaviors recorded during the daily observations.

The procedures in this phase focus on the replacement of problem behaviors with desirable behaviors. In establishing desirable student behaviors, there should be a sharp contrast between the old and the new classroom environment, which emphasizes to the student that there has been a change. Tangible reinforcers and the point system facilitate rapid improvements in student behaviors. These improvements reinforce the teacher and provide a structure within which the teacher can interact with students in a positive manner.

Phase 2: A daily E chart listing each student's name was

posted in the classroom. At the end of each day, an E was recorded here for each student who earned 17 or more points. Nothing was recorded for students who earned less than 16 points. Tangible reinforcers were no longer available on a daily basis. Instead, a student had to earn three daily E's to be eligible for an award. These three E awards consisted of assorted toys, puzzles, jewelry, and hobby and art supplies at an average cost of seventy-five cents. After a student earned 2 three E awards, he or she accumulated the daily E's for report card

E CHART

CONDUCT

LISTENING

EFFORT

PRIZE

PRIZE

STUDENT NAMES

grades. The report card categories in which students could earn E's were effort, listening, and conduct. The four point periods, teacher feedback, and the other procedures involved in the point system remained the same during this phase. Phase 2 continued for approximately three weeks. By that time, all of the students had earned at least one report card grade of E.

In this phase reinforcers that are natural to the classroom environment — grades and social reinforcers — begin to replace the tangible reinforcers. The structure of the point system still provides the teacher with opportunities to establish himself or herself as a mediator of social reinforcers.

Phase 3: After all of the students had earned at least one report card grade of E, as indicated on the E chart, Phase 3 was implemented. In this phase, two recordings of points on the student point slips were eliminated. The teacher would record the points only once before lunch and once before dismissal. However, *the teacher feedback to each student continued to be provided at all four of the scheduled times.* The teacher also continued to keep a record of student behaviors during each of the four point periods. Since two point periods passed before the teacher recorded the points earned by each student on their point slips, a student could earn two points for each of the classroom rules as indicated by the two point periods on the teacher record. During Phase 3, the students continued to earn report card grades indicated on the E chart.

When a student had earned all of the report card grades listed on the E chart, the student was told that he or she had learned good behaviors and habits, could remember how to follow the classroom rules, and did not need the E chart as a reminder. The student was informed that the teacher would keep a record of good behaviors and would periodically let him or her know how well he or she was doing and that the teacher would give each student who earned five daily E's during the week a "good note" to take home on Friday describing the student's good behaviors and progress. (*See* the good note following this chapter.) With the exception of the elimination of the two point recordings on the students' point slips and the good notes, all other procedures involved in the point system remained constant. Phase 3 continued for two weeks. By the end of Phase 3, at least half of the students should have earned all of the report card grades listed on the E chart.

The structure of the point system begins to be phased out by dropping two of the point recordings. The teacher must now provide social reinforcers — periodic words of encouragement and approval — at least twice a day without the support of the points. A variety of sources of reinforcement should be identified for the students: "*I* am proud of you." "The school *principal* will be happy to hear how well you've done." "Your *parents* will be pleased with your grades." The student should frequently be identified as a source of internal reinforcement: "*You* must be proud of yourself." "You're really learning fast." "You've done an exceptionally good job." The use of good notes provides a way to involve parents in reinforcing student improvements. Positive communication from teacher and parents to students is essential for developing student self-management skills.

Phase 4: The E chart was no longer used. The teacher no longer made recordings on the student point slips. Instead, before lunch and again at the end of the classroom day, all students recorded on their own point slips the number of points that they thought they had earned. The teacher, however, still circulated through the classroom to provide verbal feedback to each student at the four scheduled times. This feedback was based on the recordings the teacher continued to make on the teacher record. At the end of the classroom day, the students totalled their points and handed in their point slips if they had earned 17 or more points.

If the teacher's record corresponded, within reason, to the student's self-rating, the teacher would initial the point slip and return it to the student. The students could then use these initialed point slips as tickets to participate in activities as they became available. For example going on a field trip might require four initialed point slips, delivering messages for the teacher might require one initialed point slip, viewing a movie might require three point slips, being class monitor for a day might require two point slips. Students continued to earn good notes each Friday if they earned five daily E's during the week. Phase 4 continued for three weeks. During this phase, the occurrence of undesirable student behaviors should have remained under 5 percent as reflected by the data collected during classroom observations.

The procedures in this phase further deemphasizes the point system by shifting much of the responsibility of monitoring student behaviors onto the students themselves. Monitoring their own behavior through recording points earned is a step towards teaching students self-management skills. Self-management, the students' ability to engage in appropriate behaviors for extended periods of time without the continual support of external cues and reminders, still must be intermittently reinforced by the teacher. Positive teacher-student interactions must be provided in order to maintain desirable student behaviors and develop student self-management skills.

Phase 5: After a student had earned ten initialed point slips, he or she received a certificate of merit. The student was told that he or she had learned to manage his or her own behavior and no longer needed the point slips as reminders to behave properly. These students were also told that the teacher would continue to circulate through the classroom, once in the morning and once in the afternoon, to provide feedback on their classroom behaviors. Activities were still provided to the class as a whole as well as to individual students as reinforcers for good classroom behaviors. Students with certificates of merit no longer needed initialed point slips to participate in the activities. Similarly, good notes were still sent periodically to parents. In this phase, positive teacher-student interactions, which should have been developed in the previous phases, became the primary source of reinforcers for maintaining desirable student behaviors. The procedures of this phase continued throughout the remainder of the academic year.

In this phase, the cues and consequences maintaining desirable student behaviors are those natural to most classroom settings. As a result of the consultation, the teacher should have developed skills in managing the behaviors of present and future students. The students should have learned appropriate classroom behaviors that will assist them in progressing in present and future classes.

SUMMARY OF PHASES

Phase	Approx. Weeks	Point Slip Recordings	Reinforcers
1	2	4	Daily Tangible Social
2	3	4	Daily E's, Intermittent Tangible Report Card Grades Good Notes Social
3	2	2	Daily E's Report Card Grades Good Notes Social
4	3	2 (student self-recordings)	Activities Good Notes Social
5	continued through school year	none	Social Good Notes Activities

The consultant should realize that each phase is an approximate point at which a classroom management program may be started. Depending on the severity of student problem behaviors and the teacher's current skill level, it may not be necessary to begin a management program with the use of tangible reinforcers. The program may focus instead on activities, grades, good notes to parents, or solely on social reinforcers through teacher-student interactions to solve student behavioral problems.

PROCEDURES FOR EXCEPTIONALLY GOOD AND DISRUPTIVE BEHAVIORS: Students could earn bonus points for exceptionally good behaviors. They also could lose points by being fined for severely disruptive behaviors.

Bonus points for good behaviors: During Phases 1, 2, 3, and

4, the teacher could at any time record a bonus point on the student's point slip. Bonus points, which were given *immediately* after the occurrence of *exceptionally* good student behaviors, allowed the teacher to immediately recognize and reinforce exceptional improvements in a student's behavior that exceeded the teacher's expectations. A bonus point could be given on an individual or group basis. However, only one bonus point could be given at a time, and a student could not be given more than two bonus points per day.

Fines for disruptive behaviors: The teacher followed this sequence of procedures when disruptive behaviors occurred.

1. *Ignore:* Student behaviors that were not excessively disruptive to other students were ignored by the teacher. The student's disruptive behavior would subsequently be reflected by a decrease in the number of points the student earned for following the classroom rules. Disruptive student behaviors should be ignored when possible.
2. *Warn:* When disruptive student behaviors interfered with the functioning of the class, the disruptive student was warned by the teacher that if he or she continued to be disruptive he or she would be fined 2 points. If the student stopped, no fine would be recorded. However, the student's behavior would be reflected by a decrease in the number of points the student earned for following the classroom rules.
3. *Fine:* If a student continued to be disruptive after being warned, the teacher would record a 2 point fine immediately on the student's point slip and the teacher record. Fines should not be used vindictively. Once the teacher decides that a fine should be assessed, it should be recorded with a minimum of emotional exchange between the teacher and student. Fines should be used sparingly; excessive use of fines will blunt the positive value of earning points.
4. *Time-out:* If after being fined a student continued to be disruptive, the student would be removed from the classroom for fifteen minutes. During this time, the student would sit in the principal's office facing the wall and

would *not* be allowed to talk, run errands, etc. (*See* example of a time-out slip following this chapter.)
5. *School policies:* For behaviors that could be injurious to somebody or something or were in violation of school policies, the student was taken to the principal's office and regular school policies were followed. Examples of student behaviors that might result in this action include fighting, destruction of property, and leaving the room without permission.

The use of the point system served four primary functions:
1. It provided a means of recognizing and motivating student improvements.
2. It obligated the teacher to keep track of how each student was progressing.
3. It provided explicit feedback to each student concerning how well he or she was progressing.
4. It provided a structure within which the teacher could interact with each student to establish the teacher as a positive reinforcer.

Teacher-Student Interactions

The effectiveness of a classroom management program, particularly during the maintenance of the desirable student behaviors after tangible reinforcers have been removed, largely depended upon the teacher's interactions with the students. Based on classroom observations, the consultant continually provided the teacher with positive feedback concerning the teacher's interaction with the students. The consultant also continually supplemented the teacher-student interaction guidelines, rehearsing and role-playing positive teacher-student interactions when appropriate. When observing teacher-student interactions, the consultant noted the frequency, content, and quality of the teacher's delivery of verbal reinforcers. The teacher should frequently attend to and praise desirable student behaviors. However, the teacher should avoid frequent repetitions of what is said and to whom it is said. The content of the praise should identify the desirable student behavior that is being praised. Finally, the consultant noted the quality of the teacher's verbal reinforcers as reflected in the tone of voice and the congruence of facial expressions as well as other gestures. At the beginning of the program, the teacher was given the guidelines for teacher-student interactions. This was used as a reference for subsequent discussions between the consultant and teacher concerning the development of positive teacher-student interactions.

OUTLINES AND FORMS

The following materials were provided to the teacher to assist him or her in accurately carrying out the procedures of the classroom management program. Revisions may be necessary when classroom hours, point periods, reinforcers, etc. differ from those indicated on the outlines and forms. All of these outlines and forms were provided to the teacher at the beginning of the classroom management program with the exception of the summaries of phases 2, 3, 4, and 5 and the good notes, which were provided at the beginning of the corresponding phases. A sample letter of teacher recognition, to be given at the conclusion of the program, is also provided.

Teacher-Student Interaction Guidelines

Some considerations influencing the strength of a social reinforcer are the following:

1. Quality of reinforcer — tone of voice, the context of the presentation of praise, etc.
2. Quantity of reinforcer — frequency, repetitiveness, etc. If a teacher praises students in the same manner (same tone of voice, same words, etc.), this repetitive praise will become less reinforcing. The teacher should vary the types of praise that he or she uses (pat on the back, handshakes, smiles, "I like the way . . ." "This is a good example of . . ." "Good!" "That's right!" etc.). Prior accessibility also effects the strength of reinforcers. Students may not work to earn an activity period if they can participate in the activity anyway.
3. Contingency — the student must be aware of the relationship between behavior and the social reinforcer. Consistency in the expectations of the student, consistency in carrying out the various aspects of the point system, and consistency in the type of interaction the teacher has with the students help the students develop a clear awareness of what is expected of them, thus promoting the formation of habitually good classroom behavior.

Guidelines for Teacher-Student Interaction

1. Each student starts out fresh everyday. Whatever happened the day before should have been dealt with then. If it was not, there is no use dealing with it today. Reminding a child that you are mad at him for yesterday's behavior may only cause him to act up today.
2. Pay attention to students who are on task and behaving appropriately by frequent verbal praise and physical contact. Spend more time with good students than with bad students.
3. Ignore students who are not on task or who are not behaving appropriately whenever possible. Students who are

not behaving properly should not be verbally abused by referring to them as clowns, nuts, disturbed, stupid, etc.
4. Be consistent in carrying out program procedures or promises made to students. Similarly, the teacher should not make threats or promises that he or she cannot or does not intend to carry out.
5. Give the students explicit instructions on what they are to do. These instructions should be reviewed so that there is no need for individual students to ask procedural questions about what they are to do.
6. Have something for the students to do at all times. Start assignments immediately to avoid the students becoming distracted. Have supplementary material for students who finish their assignments early.
7. The teacher should call on or respond to only those students who raise their hands. No student should be allowed at the teacher's desk without permission.
8. Use other students as examples of good behavior. However, do not continually use the same student as the example.
9. When correcting student work, mark the ones that are correct rather than the ones that are wrong.
10. Individualize assignments or evaluate each student's work individually as much as possible so that each student will experience some degree of success.
11. Do not use or threaten to use academic subjects as punishment for bad conduct.
12. When the class in general is quiet, praise the entire class for their good behavior.
13. Notes to parents citing exceptional improvements of a student are desirable.
14. Classroom rules should be frequently reviewed with student participation. Show students the awards for that day. Ask students if they will get an E today. Review the point system and rules with students. Have students give examples of how they follow the rules.
15. Certain situations develop frequently in classroom settings. The teacher should be aware of these situations and respond to them quickly and consistently. The manner in

which the teacher handles common situations will greatly affect the success of the program.

TYPES OF SITUATIONS

A. The classroom is quiet — all students are working. The teacher should praise the class in general — "This is the best class in the school." "Everyone is working so hard." "Everyone is really improving in math." "This class was complimented again today for its good conduct by. . . ." Praise given to the students should be sincere and enthusiastic.
B. Most of the class is quiet but a few students are not. The teacher should ignore the disruptive student, if possible. Attention should be devoted to the well-behaved students praising them individually for not being distracted and for their good work.
C. The class is generally disruptive; only a few students are working quietly. The teacher should focus attention on the students who are working, using them as examples of good behavior. The teacher might say, "I am happy with the way . . . is working quietly." If the disruption persists, the teacher may stop the class and review the classroom rules. The teacher should acknowledge students as they become quiet and start to work.

PROCEDURES FOR DISRUPTIVE BEHAVIORS

1. Ignore.
2. Warn.
3. Fine.
4. Time-out.
5. Refer to school policies.

A Classroom Management Program 113

Instructions for Using the Teacher Record and Point Slips

The teacher record, a daily record of each student's behavior, is used by the teacher to determine the number of points each student has earned each day during each of the four point periods.

A new record is used at the beginning of each day. The date is recorded on the top of each record and the name of a student is written above each set of boxes, reflecting the seating arrangement of the classroom. Each set of boxes on the teacher record corresponds with the arrangement of boxes on the students' point slips. The letters along the left side of the set of boxes indicate the classroom rules: IS = in seat, BQ = being quiet, RH = raising hand, WH = working hard, and IO = ignoring others. T = the total number of points earned by a student during a point period for following these classroom rules.

Student's Name

IS				
BQ				
RH				
WH				
IO				
T				

The numbers across the top of the boxes indicate the four point periods in the classroom day.

The letters down the last column on the right side of the boxes represent the following: PE = the total points earned during the four point periods at the end of the classroom day, B = the number of bonus points earned during the day, F = the number of points lost because of fines during the day, G = the total number of points a student has at the end of the day adding the bonus points and subtracting any fines (this number

Student's Name
```
      1 2 3 4
   IS □□□□
   BQ □□□□
   RH □□□□
   WH □□□□
   IO □□□□
   T  □□□□
```

determines whether a student is eligible for an award or grade of E for that day).

Student's Name
```
      1 2 3 4
   IS □□□□    PE
   BQ □□□□
   RH □□□□    B
   WH □□□□
   IO □□□□    F
   T  □□□□    G
```

The teacher should have the teacher record with him or her at all times to record problem student behaviors whenever they occur.

When a student violates one of the classroom rules, a slash mark (/) is placed in the appropriate column (reflecting the

Bill
```
      1 2 3 4
   IS □□□□    PE
   BQ /□□□
   RH □□□□    B
   WH □□□□
   IO □□□□    F
   T  □□□□    G
```

A Classroom Management Program

point period in which the violation occurred) next to the classroom rule that was violated. For example, a slash mark is placed as follows for Bill who is noisy during the first point period.

If this student gets out of his seat without permission during the second point period, it would be recorded as follows.

Bill

	1	2	3	4	
IS		/			PE
BQ	/				
RH					B
WH					
IO					F
T					G

If Bill got out of his seat a second time during the second point period, this would be recorded as shown below.

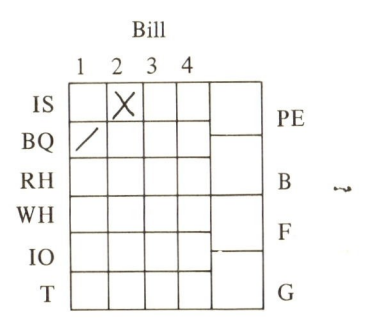

Bill

	1	2	3	4	
IS		X			PE
BQ	/				
RH					B
WH					
IO					F
T					G

If Bill got out of his seat again, this time during the third point period, it would be recorded as in the following teacher recording.

When the teacher records the occurrence of a problem student behavior on the teacher record, this record should cue the teacher to look for and praise students who are behaving appropriately. Praising good student behaviors may cue problem students to correct their behavior.

Recording points on student point slips provides a structure

```
            Bill
         1  2  3  4
     IS [  ][X ][/ ][  ]  PE
     BQ [/ ][  ][  ][  ]
     RH [  ][  ][  ][  ]  B
     WH [  ][  ][  ][  ]
     IO [  ][  ][  ][  ]  F
     T  [  ][  ][  ][  ]  G
```

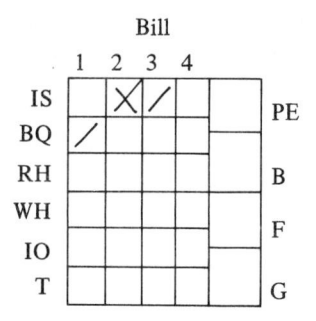

within which the teacher can establish himself or herself as a positive social reinforcer. When recording points on point slips, the teacher should not emphasize the number of points a student earns; rather, the teacher should concentrate on providing the student with positive feedback concerning his or her behavior.

Points earned by following the classroom rules are recorded by the teacher at each student's desk at the end of each point period. The recordings in the appropriate point period column are used to determine the number of points a student has earned.

If there is no slash mark on the teacher record next to a classroom rule, the student has earned a point for following that rule during that point period. While recording the point on the student's point slip, the teacher should tell the student what he or she has done to earn the point and praise the student's behavior.

A slash mark next to a classroom rule indicates that the student violated the classroom rule once during that point period. The student would still earn a point for that rule. While recording this point the teacher would tell the student what he or she did to earn the point, praise the student for the effort, and state *expectations* of further improvement.

An X next to a classroom rule indicates that the student violated that classroom rule two or more times during the point period. The students does *not* earn a point for that rule. The corresponding box on the student's point slip is left blank. The teacher states what the student did that resulted in him or her

A Classroom Management Program 117

not earning a point and states expectations for improvement.

After recording the points earned for each classroom rule on the student's point slip, the teacher adds these points and records the total on the bottom of the student's point slip and on the teacher record.

Based on the following teacher record, Bill would have earned 5 points during the first point period, 4 points during the second period, 5 points during the third period, and 4 points during the fourth period.

Bill

	1	2	3	4	
IS		X	/	/	PE
BQ	/				
RH			/	X	B
WH					
IO					F
T	5	4	5	4	G

Both bonus points and fines should be recorded on the teacher record and on the student's point slip immediately after the occurrence of the student's behavior that warranted either of the two.

At the end of the classroom day, total the number of points earned during the four point periods, adding any bonus points earned and subtracting any fines. This total, recorded in box G on the teacher record and point slips, determines whether a

Bill

	1	2	3	4		
IS		X	/	/	18	PE
BQ	/					
RH			/	X	/	B
WH						
IO					2	F
T	5	4	5	4	17	G

student is eligible for an award or a grade of E for that day. Assuming Bill earned 1 bonus point and had one 2 point fine his record would be as shown in the preceding teacher record.

Bill's point slip would look as follows:

Name: Bill				Date: Jan 14	
CLASSROOM RULES	10:30	12:00	2:00	3:00	Points Earned 18
1. Staying in Seat	/		/	/	
2. Being Quiet	/	/	/	/	Bonus 1
3. Raising Hand	/	/	/		Fines 2
4. Working Hard	/	/	/	/	
5. Ignoring Others	/	/	/	/	Grade 17
Total	5	4	5	4	

It should be noted that there are many circumstances in which a student's behavior can be interpreted as violating several different classroom rules. A student who is talking to another is not being quiet; at the same time, this student is also not doing the class work and may be disturbing another student. On these occasions, the teacher must use discretion in deciding which rule the student's undesirable behavior should be recorded under and, thus, which rule will be emphasized to the student during the teacher's feedback. It should also be noted that the point system is intended as a means of motivating students. If a student loses too many points, the point system will lose its motivating effectiveness for that student. Here also the teacher must use reasonable discretion in assessing the adequacy of each student's behavior. A majority of students in the classroom should earn a sufficient number of points each day to be eligible for an award.

STUDENT POINT SLIP

Name:				Date:		
CLASSROOM RULES	10:30	12:00	2:00	3:00	Points Earned	
1. Staying in Seat					Bonus	
2. Being Quiet						
3. Raising Hand					Fines	
4. Working Hard						
5. Ignoring Others					Grade	
Total						

TEACHER RECORD

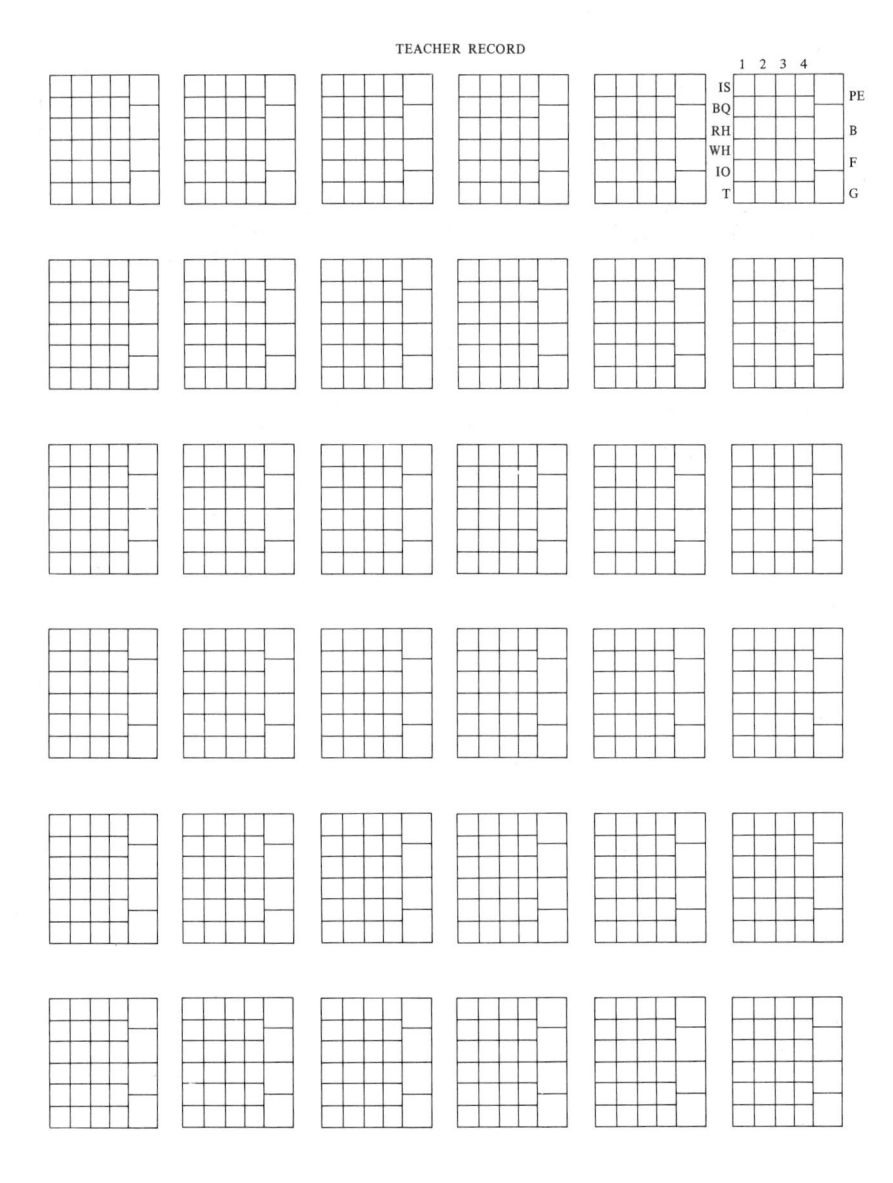

IS | | | | | PE
BQ | | | | |
RH | | | | | B
WH | | | | |
IO | | | | | F
T | | | | | G

The Day Before The Program Begins

On the day before the classroom management program is to begin, the teacher should see to the following:

1. Tell the students that they will be starting a new and enjoyable project that will be explained tomorrow morning. The project will last for two weeks.
2. Have each student move to his or her assigned seat based on a new seating chart.
3. Distribute notes explaining the program for students to take to their parents.

After school on the day before the program, the teacher should do the following:

1. Have supplementary educational materials prepared and ready for students who finish the regular class assignments early.
2. Make sure that the classroom is clean and orderly, the shelves and desks are properly arranged, and dated or unnecessary material removed from bulletin boards, shelves, etc.
3. Post the classroom rule charts and fine poster in prominent locations in the classroom.
4. Make sure that the teacher record, student point slips, and time-out slips are ready for use.
5. Have an assortment of tangible reinforcers equal to the number of students in the classroom.
6. Review and practice the introduction of the program that will be presented to the class tomorrow.

Introducing the Program

1. Have point slips on students' desks before they come in.
2. Show students the awards and tell them that you are going to explain how they can earn them.
3. Tell them that they will have a point slip everyday for the next two weeks.
4. Have students sign and date their point slip stating that this is the first thing they should do every morning.
5. Point out the classroom rule posters noting that they are the same as the ones on their point slip.
6. Explain the classroom rules to the students having them participate in a discussion of each rule (calling only on students who raise their hands).
7. Have students demonstrate following each rule.
8. Tell students that they will earn points for following the classroom rules.
9. Remind students that they *earn* points themselves; the teacher does not give them to the students, but only records them.
10. Explain the number of points that a student can earn during each rating period — 1 for each rule for a total of 5.
11. Tell the students that there are four rating periods, for a total of 20 points per day, and that they start out fresh each rating period.
12. Explain that the bonus points are for exceptionally good behavior. Bonus points are worth 1 point. Each student can receive a maximum of 2 per day.
13. Explain the fines — that they are for fighting, destruction of property, leaving the room without permission, and disturbing others. For disturbing others they will be warned first.
14. Explain the point criteria for an award (16 points) and show awards again.
15. Indicate that there is a variety of awards and that the students with the most points will select their awards first.

16. Explain to the students that they can all earn 16 points and earn an award. Each student will earn points according to his or her own improvements. Explain that they are not competing with other students, only with themselves.
17. Tell students that they will turn in their point slips at the end of each day for an award if they earned 16 or more points.
18. Emphasize to the students that if they follow all the classroom rules, the class will be a better place to learn, it will be more quiet, they will learn more and be smarter, you will be proud of them, their parents will be proud of them, etc.
19. Stress to the class that each student *earns* his or her own points by what he or she does, the teacher only records the points.
20. Review the classroom rules again, telling the students to remember when they feel like getting out of their seats that they are earning points for staying in their seats, when someone else is making noise that they earn points for ignoring him, etc.
21. Tell the students that you know that they will remember to follow the rules and that you will be proud of them.
22. Begin class assignment.

Daily Checklist

8:55 Have assorted reinforcers ready to display to the class.
Have point slips on each student's desk before class begins.
Have lesson plan prepared with supplemental material available.

9:00 Have students put name and date on point slips.
Show awards to the students indicating that the students earning the most points will have first choice.
Explain classroom rules and have students demonstrate following them.
Explain point system, fines, bonuses, and the criteria for awards.
Ask how many students will get an award today.
Begin class assignment.

9:30 Continually check classroom conduct and praise students for their improvements.
Make notations of each student's behavior throughout the day on the teacher record.
A bonus point is available for particularly good student behaviors.

10:20 Using the teacher record, begin the recording of points earned by each student on his or her point slip and provide each student with positive feedback.

10:30 Remind students that they are still following the classroom rules while lining up for recess.
Washroom/Recess

11:00 Remember to look for and praise students for their good behaviors (individually or as a group when appropriate).

11:50 Begin point recordings (remember to note improvements).
Use Teacher Record.

12:00 Lunch

1:00 Have assignments for class ready and begin immediately.
Remind students that they are following the classroom rules.
Continually make notations of student behaviors on the

A Classroom Management Program

teacher record.
- 1:30 Look for students to praise.
- 1:50 Begin point recordings (praise improvements).
- 2:00 Washroom/Recess
- 2:30 Praise students for their improvements (individually or as a class).
  A bonus point is available for particularly good behavior.
- 2:45 Begin point recordings (provide positive feedback).
  Total students' points on teacher record sheet and student point slips.
- 2:55 Have students clean up the areas around their desks before awards are presented.
  Call students who have earned 16 or more points to receive their awards.
  Students with the most points are called first.
  Have students turn in their point slips in exchange for awards.
  Congratulate students as they receive awards.
  Students should line up for dismissal after receiving their award.
- 3:00 Dismissal

Procedures for Daily Award Presentation

1. Awards should be separated into lots equal to the number of students in the class and kept in a securely locked cabinet or closet.
2. Approximately ten minutes before the end of the school day, announce to the class that awards will be distributed when everyone is seated quietly. Wait until the entire class is ready, pointing out individuals or rows that are good examples of sitting quietly.
3. Praise the students for having had a good day, making specific references to the classroom rules. Place the tray or box of awards on a desk or table in the front of the classroom so selection will be simple and quick when students come up to choose their prizes.
4. Remind the students that when they have chosen their awards, they must put them in a pocket and not play with toys or eat candy until they have left the classroom. After receiving their awards, they are to line up for dismissal.
5. Using the teacher record, students should be called to select their awards. The student with the highest point total will come up first to choose an award. If several students are consistently tied for highest total, vary the order in which they choose awards from day to day so one student does not always go first. If there are many students tied at each score, you could alternate between boys choosing first one day, then girls the next.
6. You may wish to call the highest point earners each day the "superstars" or have the class applaud as students who earn the highest number of points come up to choose their awards. As each student comes up to choose an award, praise his or her good behavior, cue specific behaviors for the next day, perhaps shake hands or give a pat on the back. If a student dawdles over choosing an award, remind the student that he or she has five seconds to pick one then count out loud to five. (No one ever fails to pick something as the teacher reaches five!)
7. Collect the student's point slip when he or she comes up to

select an award. When all award winners have made their selections, collect point slips from those not winning awards. (All point slips should be destroyed at the end of each day. The teacher record should be saved.)
8. Praise the class for having a good day. Remind them that tomorrow is a new day and everyone starts off fresh, that everyone can win an award by following the classroom rules, and that they are learning and behaving well and are good students and should be proud.

Summary of Phase 1

CLASSROOM RULES

1. In seat facing front
2. Being quiet
3. Raising hand
4. Working hard
5. Ignoring others

Each student can earn 1 point for each rule during each point slip recording.

Point Slip Recordings are made at the following times:

10:20 (before morning recess)
11:50 (before lunch)
 1:50 (before afternoon recess)
 2:45 (before dismissal)

PROCEDURES FOR RECORDING POINTS

1. Use the teacher record to determine the points earned by each student.
2. Record points earned on student point slips at each student's desk.
3. Do not emphasize numerical value of points to students.
4. Provide each student with a brief explanation (feedback) of how well he or she followed each rule, emphasizing that the student *earns* points.
5. Feedback should be positive and should include a statement of how the student earned each point, praise for good behaviors, and a statement of expectations or encouragement when appropriate.
6. Ignore and avoid arguments with students concerning the number of points earned.
7. Make sure that the recordings on the teacher record correspond with those on the student point slips.

Bonus Points (1 point each)

There is one bonus point available in the morning and one

in the afternoon; they can be immediately recorded on a student's point slip when he or she shows exceptional improvement in behavior or work.

AWARDS

Daily tangible awards are available to each student during the first two weeks. To be eligible for an award, a student must earn 16 of the possible 22 points during the classroom day.

PROCEDURES FOR DISRUPTIVE BEHAVIORS

1. Ignore
2. Warn
3. Fine
4. Time-out
5. Refer to school policies

Fines (2 points)

Students can be fined 2 points, which are recorded on their point slips, immediately after they engage in disruptive behaviors that cannot be ignored such as fighting, destroying property, throwing objects, or leaving the room without permission.

SOCIAL REINFORCERS

The teacher should practice positive teacher-student interactions throughout the day (*see* guidelines for teacher-student interactions).

Summary of Phase 2

1. Post the E chart in the classroom at the beginning of phase 2.
2. Explain the changes to the class. Tell the students that the two week project is completed.

    Since they have been behaving so well, you would like to continue to let each student know about the improvements he or she is making.

    Each student can now earn a daily grade of E (E = excellent) as an award instead of a prize.

    An E will be placed on the E chart at the end of each classroom day for each student who has earned 17 or more points.

    Points are earned in the same manner that they have been during the past two weeks — for following the classroom rules.

    When a student accumulates enough daily E's, he or she is eligible for the award indicated on the E chart.

    When a student earns an award, he or she proceeds to work for the next award.
3. Explain criteria for awards and report card grades:

    3 E's = First tangible award (approximate value of 75¢)
    3 E's = Second tangible award (approximate value of 75¢)
    3 E's = E for effort on report card
    4 E's = E for listening on report card
    5 E's = E for conduct on report card
4. Show students the tangible awards they can select from.
5. Tell the class that this project will continue for three weeks.

Summary of Phase 3

1. Tell the students that after they earn their report card grade of E in conduct, they can earn a good note to take home to their parents each Friday, but only if they earn five daily E's during that week.
2. Read the good note to the class.
3. Explain the changes to the class.

    Points will be recorded on student point slips only twice each day, before lunch and again before dismissal, instead of the previous four times each day.

    During each of the two point recordings, a student can earn 0, 1, or 2 points for following each classroom rule. At this phase of the program, students should usually be earning 2 points for each rule.

    The 2 bonus points are still available; thus, each student can still earn a total of 22 points each day.

    Fines, as well as other aspects of the program, remain in effect.

    The teacher should still continually use the teacher record. The teacher still circulates through the classroom to provide positive verbal feedback to each student four times a day — before morning recess, before lunch, before afternoon recess, and before dismissal — even though points are recorded only at two of these times.
4. In this phase it is crucial for the teacher to engage in positive teacher-student interactions throughout the classroom day.
5. This phase of the program continues for two weeks.

GOOD NOTE

Date_____

Dear Parent,

    This week your child _____ has made a great improvement in his/her behavior and work in my class. I am proud of these improvements and know that you share in this pride. To keep you informed of your child's progress, I will send this note home at the end of each week that your child shows improvement. I hope that you will be looking for these notes and will let your child know how pleased you are when he/she gives them to you.

                               Sincerely,

                               _____
                               Teacher

Summary of Phase 4

1. Students continue to earn good notes to parents each Friday.
2. Explain the changes to the class.
   The teacher will no longer record points on the student point slips.
   Before lunch and dismissal, the students are asked to record their own points according to what they believe they have earned.
   The teacher, however, continues to use the teacher record and provides positive feedback four times a day.
   At the end of the classroom day, each student hands in his or her point slip indicating the total number of points earned. If a student's point total corresponds, within reason, to the teacher record, the teacher initials the point slip and returns it to the student.
   The student can then use the initialled point slips as tickets to participate in activities as they become available.
3. Activities (the number of tickets required may vary, one or two, depending on the specific activity):
   Movies
   Special Projects
   Field Trips
   Extra Library Time
   Hall Monitor
   Classroom Monitor
4. This phase continues for three weeks. A record should be kept of the number of initialled point slips each student has earned.

Summary of Phase 5

1. Tell the class that when a student has earned ten initialled point slips, he or she will receive a certificate of merit.
   The certificate of merit indicates that the student has learned to manage his or her own behavior.
   The student no longer needs a point slip as a reminder of the classroom rules. (Point slips will no longer be given to these students.)
   The teacher has a record of the number of initialled point slips each student has earned.
   Special activities will be available to students with certificates of merit without the need of an initialled point slip.
   Other students must still have these point slips as tickets to participate in the activities until they earn their certificates of merit.
2. The teacher still circulates through the classroom four times each day to provide positive feedback to students.
3. Skills in positive teacher-student interaction should be developed and practiced by the teacher throughout the academic year.
4. Notes to parents describing the improvements made by a student are sent when appropriate.

CERTIFICATE OF MERIT

This certifies that

_____(student's name)_____

has learned appropriate classroom behaviors and has demonstrated the ability to conduct himself/herself in the ways expected of a good student in room____ at _____(school's name)_____.

                                                  Teacher   Date

In accepting this certificate, I pledge to conduct myself in accordance with the behaviors of a good student.

                                                  Student   Date

LETTER OF TEACHER RECOGNITION

This letter is written in recognition of the achievements made by (teacher's name) while participating in the teacher training and consultation activities conducted by (the consulting program or agency name).

The following is a summary of the activities required of (teacher's name). It is hoped that this summary will be kept as a permanent part of (teacher's name)'s personnel record in recognition of the time and effort he/she has invested in the program.

The goal of the training focussed on the development of the teacher's classroom management skills that result in a decrease in the number of behavioral problems occurring in the classroom. As a result of (teacher's name)'s interest and cooperation during the consultation, this goal was successfully accomplished.

The training consisted of (number) one-hour weekly consultation sessions, which began on (date) and continued through (date). During these sessions, the principles of learning and the problem solving steps of specifying problem student behaviors, assessing problem behaviors, measuring behaviors, identifying reinforcers, establishing contingencies, and developing positive teacher-student interactions were presented through discussions, readings, films, videotapes, and practice. A classroom management program was then implemented by the teacher on (date) with the assistance of (consultant's name), the consultant, and continued through (date). Periodic classroom observations were made to assess changes that occurred in both student and teacher behaviors. The information gathered during these observations was then provided to the teacher during the weekly consultation sessions.

The classroom management program involved the establishment of classroom rules, the implementation of a point system in which students could earn points exchangeable for awards, the development of positive teacher-student interactions, and the subsequent maintenance of desirable student behaviors in a natural classroom setting. In addition to the tasks involved in implementing and maintaining this program, the teacher was also responsible for numerous procedural and record keeping tasks. These included keeping daily records of each student's behavior, preparing charts and posters, and engaging in positive teacher-student interactions.

(Teacher's name) invested a substantial amount of work and displayed dedication beyond that normally required of teachers. As a result, (teacher's name) has developed conceptual and practical skills that will assist him/her in managing problem student behaviors that may occur in the classroom.

         Sincerely,

         _____
         Consultant

Part III
Consultation Experiences

In providing school consultation, the consultant must respond to an infinite variety of situational variables. Because many of these variables are created by the personalities of the principals and teachers with whom consultation is undertaken, these variables are often difficult to define and anticipate. They are, nonetheless, a major influence in determining the outcome of consultations. It is essential that the consultant develop the sensitivities and skills necessary to work with a variety of individuals. The development of these sensitivities and skills, unfortunately, is usually the product of experience. One can, however, benefit from the experiences of others. For this reason, a hypothetical consultant's log — a composite of consultation experiences — is presented in Chapter 12 to give the consultant exposure to some of the personalities and affective components that might be encountered while providing school consultation. Teacher comments are presented in Chapter 13 to provide the consultant with a better understanding of the teacher's perceptions of the strengths and weaknesses of such a consultation. This information should assist the consultant in making appropriate revisions in his or her consultation services.

Chapter 12

A CONSULTANT'S LOG

I HAVE learned a great deal from the many different people and the variety of situations I have worked with while providing school consultation. Yet, it is very difficult to convert what I have learned into concrete principles that can easily be transmitted; there are too many variables for which to account. Each consultation experience seems to benefit the next consultation. Rather than trying to sort out these variables, a seemingly impossible task, I have decided to keep a log of my consultation experiences in the hope that this will help me understand those hazy areas that are a part of each consultation. The following log is a composite of my consultation experiences.

September 29: Writing the Proposal

Though I've written numerous proposals, I still find them difficult to write. Each school consultation demands a reassessment of the consultant's role, the consultation services to be provided, and the goals of those services — all in a manner acceptable to both the administrators of the target school and the social service agency I represent. I recall problems with previous proposals I have written. The first proposal I wrote, perhaps because it was the first, was far too broad in both its scope and terms. Of course it was misinterpreted. During the initial meeting with the school principal, I found myself dragged into discussions far from my areas of expertise, interest, and responsibilities. The principal had assumed I was willing and able to discuss the impact of the id on student misbehavior!

Overcompensating, I suppose, the next proposal I wrote was far too specific and detailed — and, as a result, far too long. This proposal was dismissed by the principal to whom it was sent because she felt it didn't begin to address the variety of behavioral problems confronting her teaching staff. Somehow she got the idea that I was trying to conduct a research project rather than provide a service. I suspect she got that idea because she never finished reading the lengthy proposal, and that was my fault. Deficits in previous proposals — the need to reflect more accurately my own competencies; the need to be detailed and specific, yet brief and to the point — now provide me with guidelines for writing the next proposal.

October 18: The First Meeting with the Principal

I sent the proposal to Mr. Wall, principal of Armour School, two weeks ago, called him a week ago to arrange our first meeting, and met him today for the first time. As with so many meetings of this sort, I expected the unexpected. I was not surprised. I arrived on time but found Mr. Wall busy attempting to mollify an angry parent. Sitting there in Mr. Wall's outer office, listening to the angry voices echoing from within, I couldn't help but recall other principals I had met. There was Mr. Block who filled our first meeting with his concerns about homosexuals and murderers. In subsequent meetings our discussions bounced from one bizarre topic to another. It was almost impossible to keep him focussed on the consultation at hand. Other principals had shown their peculiarities, too. On the one hand there was the hurried and harried principal, Mr. Top, who, as he rose to terminate our ten minute meeting, gave a vague and passing approval to my proposal, "Go ahead and do whatever it is you want to do. Sounds good to me." On the other hand, there was Dr. Gradgrind, Ph.D., who instead of discussing the proposed consultation leaned back in his chair and tried to grill me about my credentials. I recalled how important it was to have a clear agenda and goals to be achieved during these meetings.

At this time the angry parent came out of Mr. Wall's office followed shortly by Mr. Wall. After he had shown the still angry parent out, he invited me in and opened our discussion with "What can I do for you; or maybe I should ask, what can you do for me?" I sensed that Mr. Wall was still concerned about his meeting with the angry parent. Though wanting to focus on the consultation proposal, I felt it was important to recognize the principal's concern and, besides, I was a little nosy. So, I replied, "I came to discuss the consultation proposal; but it looks as though you have your hands full this morning." As I expected, Mr. Wall seemed to appreciate the opportunity to discuss his previous meeting. The parent was angry because her son, Steven, was going to be placed in a social adjustment classroom. Steven had been in and out of trouble since his first day at Armour School. "He is hyperactive, indifferent, and inattentive," Mr. Wall continued. The parent, however, blamed the school and especially Steven's teacher for not understanding him. Steven had been transferred to other classrooms in the school and had been troublesome in them, too. "He is commonly referred to as the class clown. None of the teachers want him in their rooms." Mr. Wall then suggested, with as much desperation as hope, that perhaps I might be able to help correct Steven's problems. Taking this opportunity to refer to the proposal, I noted that the proposed consultation focussed on developing a teacher's skills so that he or she could manage problem students such as Steven. I then went on to stress that it would be his teacher, not I, who would be in the best position to help Steven improve his classroom behaviors.

At last we got down to the business at hand — the services and goals outlined in my proposal. I tried to sell the program by suggesting that once a teacher had been trained in the management of problem student behaviors, then he or she could become a resource for other teachers. Not only would two or three teachers benefit from my consultation, but the whole school could, potentially, benefit from it. Mr. Wall responded very favorably to this, as I expected he would, and then, a bit unexpectedly, volunteered, "And I have two teachers, Mr. Moss and Miss Faythe, in mind who I know would benefit from your training. I'm going to get them in touch with you and have them sign up for your program." I interrupted him at this point to emphasize that a way to ensure the consultation's failure is to "draft" teachers to participate. We would get the cooperation necessary for the success of the consultation only if the teachers actually volunteered to participate. A bit more tentative now, Mr. Wall responded, "Well, I think they would be willing to volunteer. I'd certainly like to talk to them about it, but I won't coerce them." Then he went on to suggest that I present my proposed consultation services to all his teachers at the next in-service meeting. I agreed but went on to ask that he not talk with Mr. Moss and Miss Faythe until after the in-service. I wanted to be the one to introduce them to the goals, requirements, and responsibilities of the consultation. I didn't want any teachers misled about what the consultation was or what to expect from it.

As I said good-bye to Mr. Wall, I gave him copies of the consultation proposal to distribute to his teachers. I left feeling that I had achieved the goals I had set for this meeting. If all continues to go as scheduled, the initial meetings with the teachers should start in early November, two months into the school year. By November, the teachers will have adjusted to the school routines and will have a better sense of the problems occurring in their classrooms. With the consultation sessions during November and December focussing on the development of the teacher's problem solving skills, the teachers should be ready to implement a management program in their classrooms by January, after the Thanksgiving, Christmas, and New Year holidays. January, after these holidays have passed, will be a good time to implement the classroom management program since consistency is extremely important. The interruptions of these holidays — the traditional classroom preparations, decorations, assemblies, and parties — will be avoided and there will still be sufficient time to complete the management program before the end of the school year.

October 31: In-service Presentation

As part of the in-service presentation, I showed a videotape of several classrooms that I had provided consultation for. As I thought they would, the teachers readily identified with what they saw, seeing themselves and their students in the troubled classrooms that first appeared on the tape and, although some were cynical, most were genuinely impressed by the changes in student behaviors that unrolled before them. During the tape, I pointed out the student management skills that the teacher was using in her instruction; at the same time I was careful to stress how important the teacher's cooperation and investment were in the development of the skills that by the end of the tape she employed so easily. The teachers were then asked to identify some of the problem student behaviors and the changes in these behaviors that they observed in viewing the videotape. After the presentation and discussion, several teachers introduced themselves and volunteered to participate in the consultation. Miss Faythe was among them; Mr. Moss was not. I made arrangements to meet with each of them and the principal to discuss the consultation further.

November 2-7: Initial Meetings with Teachers

During these meetings I was concerned that two things were accomplished — that the separate but interdependent responsibilities of myself, the teachers, and Mr. Wall were specified and that those teachers who felt coerced to participate or who would, for one reason or another, not benefit from the consultation were screened out. Mr. Wall and I met with each of the teachers individually in order to reduce peer influence among the teachers and to allow for substitute coverage in each of their classrooms while they were at the meeting.

Our first meeting was with Mr. Moss. I was surprised to see him since he showed no interest during the in-service presentation. During the meeting he seemed most uncomfortable and nervous. As I presented an outline of the consultation, he said very little except that the principal had talked with him about the program and that it was felt he would benefit from it. What little else he did say concerned "the great amount of work that seems involved in the training" and the fact that he had "very little extra time." When I asked about problems in his classroom, he briefly replied that he had "some problems on occasion," but he thought he could handle them. It was by now obvious that Mr. Moss was not at all interested in the consultation or the development of student management skills, that he was here only because Mr. Wall had made him feel obligated to be here. Past experience has taught me that working with reluctant teachers like Mr. Moss was usually a waste of both our time. Mr. Moss would begin by finding excuses for not carrying out his responsibilities to the consultation and end up by finding a reason to end it. I was pretty sure Mr. Moss could benefit from learning student management skills but was also sure that he had no interest in learning them. His "need" was hardly sufficient for the success of the program; desire is what is important.

I decided to give Mr. Moss a way to back gracefully out of the consultation before we went any further. I stated that it was an entirely voluntary program, that it did involve a significant amount of work and commitment, that some teachers did not have the time to invest in the program, and that his reluctance was understandable in light of all the other responsibilities he must have. I knew what I was about to hear even before I heard Mr. Moss's actual words: "I'm very, very busy preparing for my class. Your training sounds interesting; yes, indeed, it does. But I don't think I can spend that much time away from my teaching. Teaching must come first, you know." A bit flushed, obviously wanting to escape, Moss rose, shook hands, and slipped away.

Certainly I was frustrated that Mr. Moss had been unable to see what to me are the obvious benefits of my consultation, but I was also relieved that I wouldn't have to struggle with him in the coming months. He is by no means the only kind of difficult teacher one encounters in this sort of school consultation, and watching him leave, I couldn't help but think of others. There is the disorganized teacher, perhaps best exemplified by a Mr. Schake I once tried to work with, a man so disorganized he couldn't even plan the most basic reading, writing, or arithmetic lessons. He wasn't aware of it, of course, but his confusion was the most disruptive force in his classroom; his students couldn't help but be indirectly influenced by him.

Unfortunately, my efforts to help him develop student management skills only further distressed this already borderline teacher. As a result, consultation sessions quickly changed into therapy sessions during which his personal problems were the subject of discussion.

Then there is the dictator, a kind of teacher typified by Miss Erie. She conducted — no, ruled — her class through punishment, threat, and force. Her students were compliant, alright, but only when she was standing directly over them. Whenever she turned her back, the class would blow up. Disliking her, her students took the least opportunity to take their revenge. She didn't like them or her job and seemed to take her frustrations out on the students by criticizing and punishing them when given even the smallest of reasons to do so. The major obstacle in the consultation with her was her conviction, after fifteen years of teaching, that commands followed by force was the only correct way to manage students.

Happily, these kinds of teachers are in the minority. Most teachers are healthy, open-minded, hardworking, and cooperative and have provided me with many rewarding experiences working with them and watching their skills improve.

The second Armour School teacher Mr. Wall and I met with was a Mrs. Hoep, teacher of the lower level fourth-grade class of thirty-two students. Mr. Wall assured me before she came in that she was very interested in receiving help. She was a new teacher, just beginning her second year, enthusiastic and trying her best but still having difficulty managing her students. Hearing this, I was optimistic. New teachers tend to be the most flexible and willing to try new classroom procedures and learn new skills.

Our meeting went well. Mrs. Hoep asked about the program's procedures, goals, duration, and her responsibilities. In time, she described some of the problems she had been having with several of her students and the efforts she had made to solve them. In passing she noted that she had some knowledge of learning principles, "positive reinforcement and the like," but that they didn't seem to work in her class. She was, however, willing to try them again. She presented herself as a generally well-trained teacher, although she did at times seem sensitive to subjects or issues that might, to her, have seemed to call her competency into question. Thus, I took the opportunity to acknowledge her training and skills and to define my quite different area of expertise — the management of behaviors of problem children. She became less defensive as she became more aware that my skills would supplement rather than duplicate hers, that ours was to be a cooperative effort. We concluded our meeting by scheduling a series of consultation sessions for Mrs. Hoep and myself. In the beginning we were to meet on Monday and Thursday after school at my office. A classroom observation was also planned for Wednesday.

Mr. Wall and I continued our meetings with individual teachers, eventually talking with six — three of whom decided to participate in the program. Mr. Chayrite, a substitute physical education teacher assigned to teach the boys' social adjustment class, desperately wanted help. He had been assigned to this class of twelve "uncontrollable" boys after their regular teacher, Mr. Knough, had abruptly resigned. The third teacher in the program was to be Miss Faythe, a soft-spoken woman whose tolerance for classroom frustration was quickly being surpassed. She taught a second-grade class of twenty-eight active students. Having made the necessary agreements, discussed responsibilities, and established meeting schedules, I was now ready to proceed in consultation with Faythe, Hoep and Chayrite.

November 14-18: The First Consultation Session

My first session was with Mrs. Hoep. During our meeting I intended to present the behavioral principles that would provide the foundation for the skills and procedures to be developed during the consultation. I always find this first session especially difficult, not only because the teacher and I don't know one another yet but also because my presentation is difficult to pull off successfully. It would be easiest for me if I could simply sit there and tell a teacher what I want him or her to know — lecture, in other words. But I'm aware that this is not the best way either to develop a productive relationship with the teacher or to communicate behavioral principles. Most teachers are anxious to express their concerns about their students; they don't want to hear a lecture. In fact, some are affronted that I should presume to teach them. What seems to work best is to incorporate my presentation into the discussion of the teacher's difficulties. Thus, I told Mrs. Hoep that at this meeting we would be discussing the principles underlying the consultation but that we could do this by relating these principles to some of the concerns she had about her students.

She responded that she would like to begin with Steven, one of her most difficult students. "He can't seem to sit still for even thirty seconds. He's hyper from the moment he runs in the door in the morning until he tumbles back out that door in the afternoon, and in between he's constantly getting himself in trouble. I can't even calm him down, let alone teach him anything."

It was my turn to remark that since behavior is a function of its consequences, we would have to accurately determine not only what Steven's problem behaviors are but also the cues that set the occasion for these behaviors to occur and the reinforcers that maintain them. At that I saw Mrs. Hoep's eyes go glassy; I'd lost her with my jargon but she was not about to admit it. This gave me the opportunity to go into my "What I mean to say is . . ." routine. Without missing a beat I began to define my terms, being careful all the while to clarify them with classroom examples. When I saw she was with me again, I was able to move to my second observation, noting that the classroom environment — now providing the cues and reinforcers for Steven's problem behaviors — could be restructured to promote desirable behaviors. Our first step, however, would be to accurately specify problem behaviors in observable and measurable terms. I asked her, "Can you describe some of Steven's hyperactive behaviors?"

As she described the problematic behaviors of Steven — and several other students — I began to establish my "problem list" of behaviors that were to be targeted for change. As we continued our discussion, I took great care not to reject either Mrs.

Hoep's opinions about her students or the language she used to describe their problems, but whenever possible I tried to translate her statements into observable and measurable terms. At the same time I was careful to describe to her the strengths she already had, showing her that, perhaps without being aware of it, she was already practicing some of the behavioral principles that would be the foundation for our classroom program. I have always found that remarks such as these are most important for establishing rapport with teachers and for impressing upon them the fact that a program in behavioral management is not unlike many of the things they already do in their classrooms. Beginning to grasp the principles and happy in my recognition of her strengths, Mrs. Hoep relaxed considerably; her comments became more precise, her questions more pointed.

I knew, however, that I must not let her misinterpret our growing rapport. Certainly a comfortable relationship was essential for a successful consultation, but her cooperation must not be based on "friendship." If a teacher feels that he or she is my friend rather than a colleague, he or she is likely to feel betrayed when the time comes for me to offer constructive criticism and to indicate discrepancies between the classroom management program as it has been designed and as the teacher is carrying it out. The teacher must understand that my comments and evaluations are attempts to develop classroom management skills. To maintain the focus of Mrs. Hoep's cooperation on the tasks to be accomplished, I drew our meeting to a close by summarizing the topics, procedures, and goals of future meetings and giving her some readings covering further behavioral principles. I also gave her information forms to complete — student information and problems forms, a seating chart, and a class schedule. The early completion of these forms would be one indication of the extent of Mrs. Hoep's investment in and cooperation with the consultation. As she was leaving, we scheduled a time for me to make an observation of her classroom.

My first sessions with Mr. Chayrite and Miss Faythe were adequate but not as successful as the one with Mrs. Hoep. Mr.

Chayrite was quite opinionated, often resisting my translation of problems into behavioral terms, and quick to declare what he thought was the proper way of handling student problems. It is always very tricky to tell someone like this that if their ways of handling student problems were "proper," there would be no need for a consultation. Of course, they can't be told their errors. About all that can be done at this point in the consultation is to have them describe again and again their methods of student management and the consequences of their methods, showing them indirectly that the "proper" methods are often self-defeating.

Miss Faythe, in contrast to Mr. Chayrite, seemed very dependent. She had little to say during our session, describing her class in few words and asking few questions. She seemed content to let me do the talking and probably would have been very comfortable had I lectured her for the full hour. Though she indicated that she was very willing to cooperate, I am still very concerned about her passiveness. It is not possible for me to tell this teacher how to respond to every situation that may occur in her classroom. For Miss Faythe, establishing a conceptual understanding of behavioral principles, practice in the use of these principles, and recognition of her strengths will be extremely important in building her self-confidence and getting her to become more active, within appropriate limits.

November 21-23: Initial Classroom Observations

Today I made an initial observation in Mrs. Hoep's classroom. It seems that at least once at every school where I've consulted, a teacher forgets to announce to her students that I'll be in the room. Mrs. Hoep kept that record intact. As I entered her room, she hurriedly announced to the class that "there will be a visitor in the room today" and that "he will be working and is not to be disturbed." Mrs. Hoep's introduction was certainly preferable to the introduction Mr. Chayrite gave me yesterday when I visited his room. "This man," he barked, "is here to see which of you should go to reform school!" That shut the classroom up instantly. As the intimidated students huddled silently at their desks, I knew I had little chance of sampling some of the problem behaviors that were previously discussed. Only towards the end of the observation period did the students begin to relax. Every so often a student would turn furtively toward me and mumble, "Go home, turkey!" The students around him would then cover their mouths to hide their chuckles. Still, the class was not nearly as disruptive as Mr. Wall, the principal, had described it as being.

Miss Faythe's class was entirely different. Her students were neither intimidated nor hostile. Inquisitive would characterize them. Throughout the observation period, students came up to me asking questions like "What is your name?" and "What are you doing?" To each I replied as briefly, quietly, and neutrally as possible, "I'm working and can't talk now." I've found that this reply — neither a direct answer to their questions nor a total refusal to answer — works best to blunt their curiosity. Nonetheless, one student kept pestering me, finally resorting to flipping small wads of paper in my direction. After the fourth or fifth wad, I had almost had enough. Nothing would have pleased me more than to grab that little kid by his shirt, turn him over my knee, and paddle his tiny behind — hardly model behavior for a consultant in classroom management. After gritting my teeth through several more barrages of paper wads, I saw that the observation period was almost over. Happily, I closed my note pad and left.

After Mrs. Hoep had introduced me to her class, she handed me a seating chart and whispered, "I hope you're ready to see a lot of action. This has been a terrible day." I sat in the back of the room and recorded my observations. Mrs. Hoep, remembering that she wasn't supposed to interact with me during the observations, refrained from any further comments. In some of the other classrooms I had observed in, it was difficult to remain a neutral observer. Some teachers had asked me to arbitrate classroom disputes, judge student art work, or watch the class while he or she went to the washroom. I refrained from these activities knowing that participation in classroom functions could skew my observations.

During the period in Mrs. Hoep's room, I was free to make

thorough notes on problem student behaviors and the ways Mrs. Hoep responded to them. Many students spent much of their time walking and even running at will around the room. Others continually chattered at each other. Above the din of the already noisy room, other students cried out, "Hey teacher!" Throughout all this, Mrs. Hoep hurried from student to student, sometimes shaking a finger in reprimand, other times trying to block out the disruptions while attempting to help a student with classwork. Students were constantly pulling on the teacher's arm to gain her attention. By the end of the day, I'm sure her left arm must have been longer than her right one. Mrs. Hoep looked exhausted. Her strained attempts to be positive and to praise students generally went unnoticied. Things were going so badly that at times I felt the urge to intervene — to tell Mrs. Hoep what was happening and what she should do. But I refrained, knowing that little of permanent value would be gained by my haphazard aid now. I decided to save my pearls of wisdom for the consultation sessions.

By the end of the observation period, I had a pretty good sample of the problems in Mrs. Hoep's room. Using my observation notes and the concerns Mrs. Hoep expressed in our previous consultation session, I will be able to establish a tentative problem list. It will not be so easy with Miss Faythe's and Mr. Chayrite's classrooms, which is why I've scheduled further observations with them. I hope that the students in these rooms will soon become comfortable with my presence. Based upon my previous experience, I expect the students to acclimate to my presence by the third observation period.

November 28: The Problem

I began this consultation session with Mrs. Hoep by asking if she had any questions about the readings I had given her at our last session. She had found the readings interesting, made a few comments about them, and seemed to understand the points made in the readings. Nonetheless, perhaps because of my compulsive nature and previous experiences with other teachers, I felt it necessary to review some of the key points in the readings

— the need for consistency, the gradual shaping of behaviors, the importance of social reinforcers, etc. Some of the previous teachers who initially indicated an understanding of these and other important points either later forgot them, misunderstood them, or overlooked their significance when it came time to apply these principles in their classrooms. After emphasizing these principles, perhaps to the point of boredom as indicated by Mrs. Hoep's yawn that she politely covered with her hand, I asked about the forms she had been asked to complete. She gave me the completed class schedule and student information forms. I thanked her for being prompt, remembering the delays and excuses I had gotten from Mr. Chayrite.

Next, we discussed what I had noted during the observation periods. I remarked that her students got out of their seats frequently to gain her attention, came to her desk often, and tugged on her arm to show her their work or to tattle on another student — "Teacher, José is writing in his book!" "Sometimes you respond to them," I continued, "sometimes you don't. Still, the students seem to think they have a better chance of gaining your attention in these ways than by staying seated and raising their hands." The need for consistency and classroom rules was made apparent.

When I concluded with these and other observations, Mrs. Hoep generally concurred, but she, as did Miss Faythe and Mr. Chayrite, occasionally offered alternative explanations for the causes of problem behaviors. All three wanted to go beyond environmental cues and consequences in their classrooms. Some of their suggestions implied a physiological basis for problem behaviors, others implied internal conflicts or bad parent and community influences. Mrs. Hoep saw all of the foregoing at work in her classroom and felt that my assessment of behavioral problems, while accurate, was oversimplified. Mr. Chayrite had, on the other hand, argued that the disruptive behaviors of most of his students were innate characteristics. "They were born that way," he grumbled in all seriousness. Miss Faythe was concerned with assigning blame and responsibility to the parents and community, noting that she was doing the very best that she could under the circumstances. Though my reply to each of these teachers varied somewhat, the basic message was the same: "There are certainly many varied and complex causes for student problem behaviors. Some lie outside the classroom setting and beyond the teacher's control. But we can at least tackle the causes that lie within the classroom and perhaps, in turn, influence some of those outside the classroom setting." With this understanding established, we continued to identify and assess the problems.

The problem behaviors identified in each classroom were essentially the same — random student movements, talking, shouting to gain the teacher's attention, other noises, grabbing at the teacher, objects being thrown through the air, fighting as well as minor scuffles, and an abundance of litter covering the classroom. What differed from room to room was the severity — the frequency, duration, and intensity — of these problems and what the teachers did or didn't do that contributed to their occurrence. With the problem behaviors now identified, I can now proceed to measure the severity and changes in these behaviors during the subsequent observation periods.

December 1-3: Desirable Student Behaviors

I have completed several observations in each of the three classrooms. During this consultation session with Mrs. Hoep, I reported the results of the observations made in her classroom. Her students were spending an average of 60 percent of their time, as sampled during the observations, engaged in problematic behaviors. Mrs. Hoep was not surprised, remarking that she thought it would even be greater.

After explaining the observation procedures and reviewing some of her strengths and how they could be used in addressing the student problems that were observed, we turned to a discussion of student behaviors that she wanted to see replace the troublesome ones. Mrs. Hoep desired that the students "stay in their seats, be quiet, do their work, and learn something." These desirable behaviors will provide the basis for defining the classroom rules.

Mr. Chayrite and Miss Faythe eventually noted similar desired behaviors. It was difficult, however, to get Mr. Chayrite to specify them. His first response was "I want the students to straighten up and act right." I had a different problem with Miss Faythe. She wanted her students to learn from each other in an "open classroom" setting and didn't want the students to sit doing their work like robots. After discussing the need to teach students prerequisite behaviors before they could be expected to behave appropriately in an open classroom, she agreed to look at establishing an "open classroom" as a long-term goal to be addressed after the students learned the prerequisite behaviors.

December 5-14: The Plan

I and my Armour School teachers were ready to consider the procedures to establish desirable student behaviors. Our discussions of the contingent relationships between desired behaviors and positive reinforcers and of the behavioral criteria for earning awards went well for two sessions — probably because the terminology was new to the teachers. But with the third session on this subject, I began to sense some hesitancy, even resistance, in my three teachers. It was blunt Mr. Chayrite who brought the issue into the open. As I was trying to make a particular point about positive reinforcers, he interrupted, blurting, "But that's bribery! You're telling me I'm supposed to pay my students for something they should be doing anyway! I expect my students to do what's right because it's right, not because they're going to get some kind of toy!" "Ah, the old ethical dilemma," I thought to myself. As so many other teachers had been, these, too, were concerned about the ethics of behavioral change. In my session with Miss Faythe, she was equally troubled but put her case more delicately. "Isn't this manipulation?" she asked. "Aren't we imposing our value systems on the behaviors of our students?" Mrs. Hoep saw the other side of the coin and was concerned not so much with what she would be doing but with what she would not be doing as she implemented the program: "I think the students will get away with murder. You're telling me what to do when things go right — reward my students, and such. And that's all very nice, but what am I supposed to do when things don't go right?"

After hearing each of them out, I responded with what I have come to call my "save the children" speech. I began by telling them that the procedures they would follow are intended to teach their students behaviors that will help them progress socially as well as academically. "What we're trying to do is ethically as well as educationally and psychologically sound. Learning how to behave in the ways expected of them will provide students with alternatives to being disruptive, but we are not forcing them to behave in a certain way. They have the choice — more choices, I might add, than they had in their old, unstructured classes. We do hope, however, that the students will become aware of the advantages of behaving properly — face it," I tell my teachers, "someone must decide what 'proper' means, and it might just as well be us since we already make similar judgements that affect each student's progress in school."

I then went on to point out to each that there are always consequences for student behaviors, consequences when the behaviors are proper, consequences when they're improper. We need to recognize this fact and take advantage of it. When we restructure a classroom environment, we try to make the desired behaviors more reinforcing for the students than the undesirable behaviors. We do this by restructuring consequences, by providing students with productive ways of getting what they want — attention, recognition, rewards, or whatever. But I reminded them that tangible rewards are not given out forever; they are phased out in favor of social reinforcers, the very same kind of reinforcers we adults expect as our due for a job well done.

I emphasized to Mrs. Hoep that this program does not neglect a child when he misbehaves. Procedures for ignoring inappropriate behavior, response cost, time-out, and adherence to school policies are as important to this program as the procedures for reinforcing appropriate behavior. I then reminded her of the dangers of attempting to deal with problem student behaviors in "the old way." Sure, she would see some immediate benefits by shouting at each and every misbehaving child, "Sit down, shut up, and get to work!" She'd release some nervous energy and her students would be intimidated to silence — for a few minutes anyway. But she also had to recognize the long-term consequences of classroom management, or mismanagement, by decibel level and emotional outburst. The children had learned that they could gain her attention through movement, noise, and irritation. Having gained that consequence through these behaviors before, they would try it that way again. The teacher must learn to ignore disruptive behaviors whenever possible rather than inadvertently reinforcing them. Doing this requires consistency and patience from the teacher since the students will, at times, try the old way of getting what they want, testing the teacher and exploring how much they can get away with. I recognize that punishment is sometimes appropriate and effective. However, I seldom tell this to the teachers since, in some cases, teachers will take this to be a sanction of the use of excessive punishment. When teachers are not told that punishment is occasionally useful, they are more likely to think of positive alternatives.

If my "save the children" speech is a success, its very success always introduces one danger — that the teachers will come to expect too much too fast from a management program. Too many teachers come to expect perfection; they expect that their students will become quiet, attentive little scholars overnight. When at the end of my speech to Miss Faythe I saw her enthusiasm becoming overenthusiasm, I had to caution her that behavioral change would be gradual. Some students would adapt to the program more quickly than others. Her students would arrive where she would like them to be through shaping, gradually increasing the criteria for reinforcement. Miss Faythe seemed deflated by my words, but she also admitted that I was right and continued to say that she could see how setting her own expectations too high early in the program might be one way of sabotaging all her efforts.

In the following meetings with each teacher we discussed the paperwork involved in the consultation — the point slips, teacher record, and time-out slips. Sitting there with a sheaf of sample forms on her lap, Miss Faythe was thoroughly befuddled. "Let's see," she mused, "I should pass out the time-out slips — no, the point slips — and record the classroom rules. No, wait..." But five minutes later, she had everything straight and was relaxed again. When I passed out the sample forms to Mr. Chayrite, he kept thumbing through the stack as I talked and when I had finished explaining them grumbled about the amount of time it would take to record points on *both* the students' point slips and the teacher record. I found myself wondering as he talked, if he were any relation to his colleague, Mr. Moss. Mrs. Hoep understood the forms well enough but was skeptical. "Do you think," she asked, "that all these slips of paper and little slash marks will really make a difference?" I assured her they could and once more explained why and how.

At the end of this session I cautioned each teacher not to implement any of the procedures we had discussed in this and earlier meetings until they had had a chance to practice implementing them and were ready to implement the entire program. Some teachers want to begin now, this instant, even though they don't fully understand the entire program. Others seem to treat the program as if it were a smorgasbord or a Chinese menu — a little bit of this, a little of that, a dab of positive reinforcement, and just a pinch of time-out. Still others want to implement each new procedure as they learn it — the classroom rules today, point slips a few days later, and awards a few days after that. Invariably, however, the students acclimate to the gradual changes that such haphazard applications introduce and the disruptive behaviors continue as before. If anything, such behaviors become more difficult to control. Thus, I stressed that we are involved in a program and must proceed in a planned, systematic way.

December 18 to January 4: Practice

We have spent the past two sessions practicing the implementation of the program, particularly the teachers' presentation of the point system to the students, the recording of points earned by a student on the teacher record and student point slips, the presentation of awards at the end of the classroom day, and positive teacher-student interaction. All three teachers were at first very reluctant to role-play, even though I had spent parts of many previous sessions posing hypothetical situations — "What if a student . . . ?" "How would you answer if . . . ?" — to which they had to respond as they would in the classroom. But there's a great difference between role-playing as part of an on-going discussion and role-playing as if one were on stage, pretending that I and the wall behind me are a class full of students. To put each of the teachers more at ease, I told them that I would begin by playing the role that they would soon play in the classroom and that when I had finished, they could practice imitating me. I always find that when I model a classroom situation I remember and then emphasize those "little" things that so often get lost in the discussions of principles, forms, and procedures but that are vital to the success of the program, things like tone of voice, ways of giving social reinforcers, ways of handling particular kinds of students.

I began by presenting the point system to my imaginary class, gaining their attention by first showing them the awards they could earn. I stepped out of character for a moment to tell each of the teachers that such a display was especially effective in gaining the attention and cooperation of highly disruptive classes. The students would know from the first minute what they could work for. Stepping back into character, I told my class that they were going to start a new program in which each student could earn one of these awards and I would tell them about the program as soon as all students were sitting quietly. After explaining the classroom rules and point slips, I asked some of my students to demonstrate how they could earn points by following each rule. I asked others to comment on how well these students were following the rules. I asked still others to show how they would not earn points by failure to follow one of the rules. If my teachers are warming to my performance by the time I get to student role-playing, I ask them to pretend to be the students. Often when they act the role of students, they have particular students in mind and anticipate actual situations, actual problems, that will occur when they implement the program in their rooms. The way in which I, as the teacher, handle them, helps provide them with suggestions for dealing with the students they have in mind.

Following this part of my demonstration, I reminded the teachers that they should review the point system at the beginning of class *every* day for the first week of the program and twice a week thereafter. I also told them to tell their students that this new program would end in two weeks. Knowing this, the students would be much more likely to see subsequent changes in the point system as added features rather than as the removal of reinforcers. But above all else, I stressed, the students must see the program as fun — an enjoyable way for them to *earn* awards by learning and practicing good behavior.

Next, I modeled point recordings, reminding the teachers that they should carry their teacher record with them at all times. Without these records they would not be able to record continuously the occurrence of problem behaviors during each period. After showing them how I kept my records, I went on to demonstrate how, at the specified time, to record on the students' point slips the number of points they had earned. As I recorded points on sample slips I was careful to emphasize desirable student behaviors. With each of my students, I tried to find another way to express my praise; after all, "very good" can quickly come to sound very monotonous and mechanical and kids pick this up very quickly. I also described in detail what each of my students had done to earn his or her points so that the teachers would see the importance of accurate feedback to their students. The children must know exactly what they did to earn points. Stepping out of character again for a moment, I warned the teachers against emphasizing the number of points a student earns. To emphasize the number of points is to fix in student minds a correlation between that number and the required behavior; this makes it more difficult later on when the point system is changed. Even worse, some students try to argue for more points or blame others for the fact that they only got one point instead of two. Back in character once more, I came to a student who had earned only two points for this marking period. I did not reprimand or shame him; instead, I stated as clearly as possible exactly what the child had to do to earn all his points during the next period. Ignoring his angry outburst — which Mrs. Hoep acted out for me — I went on to my next imaginary student.

Finally, I modeled the awards presentation at the end of the classroom day, after first telling the teachers that they should allow the last ten minutes before dismissal for this ceremony. By no means should the students be kept after class — late dismissal is for them a punishment that may come to outweigh the value of the awards. With this out of the way, I told my imaginary students that their awards would be given as soon as all of them were seated and quiet. Using my teacher record, I called each student up to select his or her award, beginning with the highest point earner. While passing out the awards, I was careful to provide much social reinforcement with each one. As the awards were handed out, the students got their coats and lined up for dismissal and I reminded them that they would lose their awards if they played with them while they were in school.

Having modeled what I wanted the teacher to do, I then asked the teacher if he or she would practice implementing all three aspects of the program, its introduction, point recordings, and giving out awards. Mr. Chayrite harrumphed and said, "I know what to do! I just saw how you did it. I'll do just fine in my classroom." I responded that I could certainly understand how ill at ease he must feel acting out a situation and that I was sure he knew exactly what to do, but I went on to stress the importance of getting a feel for the program, a feel for the new ways of teacher-student interaction that are required for its success. Finally, and with great reluctance, Mr. Chayrite played out his role, but he tried to rush through it and seemed concerned only with convincing me that he knew what to do and when. His trouble was that he didn't know *how* to do what he knew. Miss Faythe was reluctant too, and at first was extremely self-conscious, almost as if she were addressing a crowd of thousands with dried egg on her face. After much encouragement, however, she gradually warmed to her role. Mrs. Hoep was a delight, her tone of voice was just right, she forgot hardly a thing, and she seemed to have a knack for stressing exactly those elements of the program that were essential for its success.

As the teachers practiced their presentations, I interrupted occasionally to remind them of things they had forgotten and to indicate where further emphasis was necessary or where a shift in stress had to be made. I had to remind Mr. Chayrite, for instance, that he had to lay greater stress on student responsibility for earning awards. He wasn't *giving* awards to them, they were *earning* them. Miss Faythe I had to remind to describe accurately and fully to her students exactly what each had done to earn an award. At other times as they practiced, I pretended to be different students. Poor Miss Faythe! With her I pretended to be a student who had earned no points. After she had explained what was expected of me, I angrily wadded up my blank point sheet, threw it on the floor, and screamed, "I don't want no stupid points anyway!" I thought she'd burst into tears. It was only with difficulty that I taught her to refuse to be flustered, ignore the student's outburst, and go on to the next child. With Mrs. Hoep I pretended to be a student arguing for more points. She handled me nicely, praising me for my good behavior, ignoring my argument, and stressing what was expected of me during the next point period. She will not be one of those teachers who attempt to use points as a crutch, leaning on them for the success of the program instead of developing appropriate social cues and reinforcers.

We wound up these sessions by practicing teacher responses between those periods when points are given. I reminded the teachers to praise the whole class when all are quiet. When some are being disruptive, I reminded them to ignore their behavior, focussing instead on those who are following the rules. This they can do by asking the class, "Let's see if we can tell who is sitting quietly, working hard on his assignment." Numerous other examples were provided to stress the point that teacher praise should not be restricted to the point recording times.

January 5-9: Implementation

On the day the classroom management program is to begin I always feel that I would like just one or two more weeks to further prepare the teachers. But there's only so much that can be done in preparation, and in this instance Mr. Chayrite, Miss Faythe, and Mrs. Hoep were as ready as they ever would be. To make their first day go as smoothly as possible, I had made arrangements to spend all of it with them, observing their implementation of the program, immediately correcting any errors in their presentations, and noting any discrepancies between procedures and practice. I, of course, said nothing in the classroom, but whenever the teacher had a break, we huddled together and I gave my observations and suggestions.

Mrs. Hoep, as I had expected, did an excellent job not only of clearly presenting the point system to the students but also of selling it warmly. Mr. Chayrite, on the other hand, gave only the fuzziest explanation of how the students earned points, when the points would be recorded on student point slips, and how many points were required to earn an award. Instead of explaining the program, he stressed the rules, "You will stay in your seats! Did you hear that? Stay in your seats! You will work hard! And when I say work, I mean work. No monkey business, now!" And so on. He sounded like a drill sergeant. He got so carried away with his speech on the rules that he forgot to have students demonstrate how to follow and not follow the rules he was giving. He made the whole program sound capricious — he would *give* points when he wanted, to whom he wanted. If I were one of his students, it would not have occurred to me that I could earn points. Nor would it have occurred to me that earning these points could be fun. Miss Faythe did an adequate job. She presented the program in enough detail, but she was so nervous that she forgot certain things and had to go back. It sounded for a few minutes as if the students would get awards for which she would give them points! And with her jitters, she was not able to sell the program successfully. At the end of her presentation, the students were definitely taking a "wait and see" attitude.

Following the presentation of the program, Mrs. Hoep's room was very quiet; students sat at their desks and worked away. In Mr. Chayrite's and Miss Faythe's classrooms, the decibel level was a bit lower than usual, but there was still too much noise and too many disruptions. At the time of the first point recordings, Mrs. Hoep's children smiled and seemed to genuinely appreciate the praise and evaluative descriptions she provided. They knew that she was, in effect, telling them exactly how to earn the awards they wanted.

Some of Mr. Chayrite's students, however, seemed wholly indifferent to the points he had handed out. It was obvious they had little, if any, understanding of the effects of the points. Others — the quicker students — knew exactly what the effects of the points would be. When he said to one of them, "Look you're not getting any points because you are jumping around like a pogo stick." that student turned angrily on him, "Gimme my points! Steven punched me! Take away his points!" Mr. Chayrite didn't help matters at all when he continued the argument with "Look, who's in charge here? Did I say no point or didn't I? Huh?" Mr. Chayrite continued to use the points like clubs to hit the students on their heads with throughout the classroom day.

It took most of Miss Faythe's students until the second recording period before they began to get the idea of the point system. I was happy to see that she ignored two disruptive outbursts by students who did not receive all their points, but she was too abrupt with those who earned all of their points. She simply walked up to each student's desk, marked the points, mumbled "Very good," and then was off to the next desk. At her break I had to remind her of the varieties of praise she could give; I also reminded her that she would find it much easier to record points if she kept her teacher record with her at all times.

At the end of this first day Mrs. Hoep's children actually applauded each other excitedly as one by one they walked to the front of the room to select their awards. Miss Faythe's students also enjoyed the recognition, but their enthusiasm turned quickly to nervous energy because she had begun the awards ceremony too late. The dismissal bell had rung and half the class had still not selected their awards. Most of Mr. Chayrite's class booed and snickered as those few who had won awards went to the front to select them. He had been too stingy with his points and it was obvious that those who hadn't earned enough felt that the program was simply a way to identify and award teacher's pets. I had to remind him after class that the program would be successful only if a high percentage earned awards every day of the program.

January 13-19: Implementation

We are now almost at the end of the first week of the classroom management program; each of the teachers has by now formed an opinion of the program. Mrs. Hoep told me today, "It can't last. The change in my students' behavior has been too sudden, too striking. They must be under a lot of pressure — tension — trying so hard to do their work and be good. One of these days they're going to explode." I assured her that the program was only doing what it should do, that there would be no major explosions, and that she had demonstrated time and again that she could easily handle any minor eruptions. However, I reminded her that there would still be good and bad days in the classroom, as there always are.

Miss Faythe had seen only a little change, had tried very hard, and was very disappointed. Though her students were behaving somewhat better, she was afraid the program wouldn't work. To her I replied that she just had to give it, herself, and her students time. I told her that it would probably take her a little bit longer to bring about the desired changes in her students. Because she is still not at ease with the program and having trouble implementing it, I asked her to extend the first phase for another week. Tomorrow she is to tell her class that because the students were trying so hard, the program will be extended for one more week. This extra week will give me more time to role-play with Miss Faythe and build her confidence in her ability to handle her class. When both she and her class are ready, I'll ease them into phase 2. They might be behind Mrs. Hoep and her class, but time is not nearly so important as effective management at each stage of the program.

If Miss Faythe feared the program would not work, Mr. Chayrite was *sure* it would not, and he had a week's worth of failures as evidence to prove it. It didn't matter, as I tactfully tried to remind him, that he did not carry out all the procedures involved in the point system even though prodded time and time again, that he refused to ignore disruptive behavior, that he looked upon points as gifts rather than as earned, that he had been inconsistent in all aspects of the program. None of this mattered to him; the fault lay entirely with the program. What he did not say, of course, was that he had done everything to ensure the failure that both of us recognized. I was not surprised when he finally announced that he was "getting out of the program" in order to "concentrate on teaching." I was sad to see him withdraw from the program after all the work in preparing for it and sad, too, for his students, but I knew that there would be no changing his mind.

January 23 to March 15: Implementation

I proceeded in consultation with Faythe and Hoep. Mrs. Hoep had developed a good grasp of the teacher-student interaction skills that are so important in managing student behavior. What at one time seemed to her to be superficial now came very naturally. She now effortlessly praised students, modeled good behavior, and recognized gradual improvements. She, in turn, was very reinforcing to myself. During the consultation sessions she noted how much more competent she felt as a teacher and that she was now actually teaching and enjoying it. Other times she would note the changes in her students. "Not only have their behaviors improved, but they seem to be happier. One student, Gwendolyn, actually smiles now. She never smiled before."

Mrs. Hoep, with only a little hesitancy, proceeded through the next phases of the program during which the tangible reinforcers and then the points were removed. Things went smoothly during each transition to the next phase. This was a relief for myself as well as for Mrs. Hoep. I recall a previous consultation experience where the teacher, thinking that everything was under control in his classroom, terminated the consultation before the tangible reinforcers were removed and before his teacher-student interaction skills were sufficiently developed. Sure, the students were behaving exceptionally well in his classroom, but they were doing so to earn tangible reinforcers. Since this teacher had not yet developed his skills in delivering the social reinforcers that would replace the tangibles, shortly after the termination of the consultation his students became as disruptive as before. This teacher had fallen back on his old unsuccessful ways of managing his class. This was not the case with Mrs. Hoep. She accepted her success gracefully; though concerned about whether or not each phase would be effective, she eagerly continued, making the appropriate changes. About five weeks and several phases into the program, desirable student behavior continued to be maintained and the class began to participate in more spontaneous learning activities. During one of the sessions Mrs. Hoep noted the time when her class visited the honors class. "My students were so proud of themselves. They used to think of themselves as the dummies, but when they found out that they were ahead of the honors class in their math workbook they boasted about how smart they were."

Miss Faythe was now also enjoying success in her classroom. Though she didn't have as good a grasp of the teacher-student interaction aspects of the program as did Mrs. Hoep, her students continued to improve. There were two students that Miss Faythe saw notable changes in. Bill, the class brute, no longer pushes, shoves, or bruises other students. Valery, previously known as motor-mouth, still likes to talk but most of the time she waits to talk when it is appropriate to do so. These and other changes were very encouraging to Miss Faythe. The data I collected during the classroom observations, which I graphed, further supported Miss Faythe's perceptions of gradual positive changes that were taking place in her classroom.

When after several weeks Miss Faythe's children began to behave well consistently, I began to concentrate on further developing her skills in socially reinforcing these behaviors so that eventually she could remove the tangible reinforcers. As she saw the program working, her confidence in her own skills increased and, as they did, she was able to act more effectively as a positive reinforcer for desirable behaviors. She was nervous and hesitant when, after the several weeks of success with them, I told her it was time to remove the tangible reinforcers. She was, of course, reluctant to give up her crutches — tangible reinforcers and points — but I gave her much encouragement and told her exactly how to prepare her class for each change. She was surprised and delighted to see how favorably her students responded when she told them that the program would continue but that they would now earn report card grades and good notes to take home to their parents. And she was nervous again two weeks later when it was time to de-emphasize the point system and nervous a third time when she eliminated the point recording periods entirely, but she had so developed her skills in social reinforcement that she was able to bring off both program changes with few problems. What made each change easier of course was the fact that her children were not only well behaved but saw themselves as well behaved. Their self-images had changed along with Miss Faythe's.

April 20 to May 4: Termination

I am now at the end of my consultation with the two teachers at Armour School. I feel my stay here has been a success. Miss Faythe and her class remained a week to two weeks behind Mrs. Hoep and her class throughout my consultation, but gradually Miss Faythe developed her confidence both in the program and in her skills. Miss Faythe's efforts never flagged, and now she is almost as skillful in classroom management as Mrs. Hoep. Both Miss Faythe and Mrs. Hoep are now able to conduct ordered classes that are academically stimulating, classes where the children not only learn — some for the first time — but enjoy doing so, free from the distractions and chaos of the old days. I don't mean to imply that all this happened without a hitch. Sure, there was a fight here and there, a few time-outs, and an occasional angry student. The teachers still will occasionally complain about problems they are having with students. However, the types of problems they now note are nowhere near as severe as they had been. Steven, still not the ideal student, no longer writes on Anita's face with a crayon, though sometimes he is caught making faces at her. Both teachers have so developed their skills that no situations are now intolerable; none of them ever get entirely out of hand.

Mrs. Hoep and Miss Faythe are no longer prison wardens — they're teachers. And just now I'm beginning to see some of the ultimate benefits of my work: A few Armour teachers have begun coming to Miss Faythe and Mrs. Hoep for suggestions about their classes; Mr. Wall, their principal, has been singing their praises to other teachers and there's even talk that Mrs. Hoep should be given the teacher-of-the-year award.

I collected the teacher comments about their consultation experiences that both teachers were asked to write. By reading them, I continue to learn how to improve my consultations.

A Postscript: On my way out of Armour School today, I happened to pass Mr. Chayrite's room. I couldn't help but hear his voice hammering through the door, "You, Alicia, keep your hands to yourself! Stop bothering Sally! How many times do I have to tell you! And you! Yes, Sammy, you! Get back over here to the reading group this minute! Can't you sit still? When will you children ever learn to behave?"

Chapter 13

TEACHER COMMENTS AND EVALUATIONS

AT the conclusion of an actual consultation program, each teacher in that program was asked for comments on and evaluations of the consultation. The following topic outline was provided for the respondent, but it was emphasized that the teachers did not need to limit themselves to this outline; it was intended only to provide suggestions.

Outline For Teacher Comments and Evaluations

1. Briefly describe problem student behaviors you are concerned with and the changes in them that may have taken place.
2. Comment on the techniques and principles that you learned and found effective in managing student behaviors.
3. Evaluate the consultation sessions, reading materials, and time requirements and suggest changes where they seem appropriate.
4. Describe changes in your feelings and behaviors as a teacher and the changes in the attitudes of your students.

Six representative teacher comments and evaluations are provided here. A careful reading of these comments should give the consultant a feeling for teacher concerns and what these teachers see as the chief benefits of school consultation. These comments should further extend the consultant's awareness of those affective elements that must be considered by the consultant when providing school consultation.

Comments by J. K.

This isn't an evaluation, just some reflections on the program, my children, and myself. At the beginning of the program, I was going to keep a diary. Unfortunately, my usual procrastinating self never did, so now I can only tell what I remember.

The first few days [of the classroom management program] I thought things were going along pretty well. There were rough spots, but things were getting better. However, you [the consultant] seemed worried because the rewards weren't having a great immediate effect.

As the weeks went on, I felt like I was trudging along. If I just kept "following the rules" pretty soon things had to get better.

I think that the third and fourth weeks were very difficult.

I was getting tired of being patted, pushed, and screamed at while I was ignoring [problem student behaviors]. I thought for sure that I was going nuts and the children were sane. I couldn't see much humor in situations anymore. It was sort of grin and bear it, with more "bear it" than grin.

During this time, you [the consultant] were a great help because you were very encouraging. You kept mentioning changes, small ones, and asking for tighter controls — for example, milk carton throwing was reduced to stamping [on the cartons] and then eliminated. I was so anxious to help you in return for all you had done that when we talked, I would try very hard to describe behavioral changes. Usually this was the first time I had spoken of them. Although I could feel changes, I didn't usually take the time to put them into thoughts; this made it more difficult for me to respond.

Next I remember two great things happening. One concerned another teacher who had been rather skeptical about the project. She commented on how much more controlled my class as a whole seemed and how the individual children seemed calmer. The second was answering one of Jennifer's questions. Suddenly I realized that she was sitting down, raising her hand! She had been one of my biggest pains in the neck.

I'm not going to say much about Steven. I think far too much time has been spent on one boy instead of looking at the thirty-one other children.

For four long years I read about and listened to lectures on developing self-awareness in children. Some great thoughts, I suppose. But it seems funny that no one ever mentioned self-awareness in teachers, especially beginning teachers. I think that the behavior therapy approach has a lot to say for itself in this regard. First, the teacher must be constantly aware of herself, perhaps more aware of herself than she is of every classroom situation (which is impossible). She has to be aware of herself because she, too, has to follow the classroom rules. Whatever the situation, she must remember that she is in control and must administer justice as fairly and consistently as possible. To do this was very difficult for me.

I had to realize that as much as I wanted it to be their classroom and a pleasant place, it was really my classroom and how I controlled things determined how pleasant it was. Schools, unfortunately, are benevolent dictatorships. After all, even the behavior rules were mine and not anything the children voted on. I'm sure their ideas of important behavior would be quite different.

Probably the most difficult thing for me was learning not to take things personally. I have always felt things when other people were hurt — stick up for the underdog, etc. But empathy is not a virtue for teachers. When Steven would strike out at someone or another student would do something incredibly cruel, I would want to strike back at the bully. I was asking the children to ignore these behaviors but not doing so myself. There was one time when I was very angry and I clamped down very hard on Steven. When I related it, [the consultant] tactfully reminded me that I was modeling aggression — which was true. But worse, I was not modeling "ignore others" or anything else I wanted them to learn.

The second kind of not-taking-things-personally is realizing that the children aren't screaming or pushing or repeating your name incessantly or pounding on your body because they *want to hurt you*. They do this because they need something and you are an object to help them attain it. Believe me, when you have a headache and are trying to ignore, thirty-two kids who are repeating your name over and over as they beat your body while you are frantically looking for the one soul who is doing his work so you can compliment him, it is very easy to become paranoid. You can easily believe that they are a terrible trained army out to get you!

I think that the program has made me realize that you are manipulating — conditioning, if you will — children to respond in a way so that you can do your job, teach or whatever. At the same time, the children try to manipulate you in ways so that they can reach their goals. The trick is to teach them to manipulate you in ways that are acceptable to you and to everyone else, i.e. by raising their hands. A lot of self-awareness came out in letters to my husband [in the Navy]; I realized from them that I had changed a great deal. I don't want to kill Steve or April or Carlos anymore, I just want them to change.

As for the children, I think even the most terrible have changed. No one pokes people with pencils and gouges out flesh, no one kicks people in the spine or throws milk cartons or crayons (well, almost never). And, at best, many behavior problem children have become model (well, almost) students. Activities in the class are generally quieter. I can hear during reading groups. Reasonable order has been instituted.

I still get exasperated and tired and cranky, but nothing is ever as bad now as I remember it once was.

I am anxious to start a program like this in the fall, when I know what I will do from the beginning and can manipulate basic learning situations. I have definite ideas about new procedures — how to begin lining up, getting coats, etc. By starting the program at the beginning of the year, I can avoid the mid-year problem of "Okay kids, let's try another new approach. We'll try this till teacher goes mad and then we'll try something else."

The only really terrible time I remember during the consultation is the week and a half when you [consultants] both went to the psychology workshop, then got sick, were busy, or whatever. It was during a program change I should have been able to handle, but it didn't work well and I was panicky. I knew something was wrong and I didn't know how to fix it or what I was doing. It may have been the on-set of spring vacation fever or getting down to the regular schedule transition, but pretty soon things were not going well. I noticed a greater frequency of negative responses, but I couldn't help it. Then it passed — thank God. I always sort of wondered if it wasn't an experiment in "don't reinforce the teacher and see what happens," because, so help me, I was following the procedure — it just didn't seem genuine. If it was an experiment, it was a classic. If not, you should think about it. You often tell me there is little in the way of teacher reinforcers and I keep saying they consist of better classes, etc.; but those are small, almost indistinct reinforcers. Perhaps the presence of someone objective who can help would be a reinforcer until the teacher is absolutely sure of herself. Such a situation would also have the rather negative but strong "someone is watching" effect that makes you want to live up to some expectation. As with kids, what good is it if occasionally you don't get a nod? Hopefully for me such an "overseer" won't be necessary in the fall. Other things will be reinforcing, like keeping my job, pleasant classes, a sense of accomplishment, whatever.

There are days now when I wonder if they (the kids) have really gone anywhere. If I think about it, I know they have. But it seems that there is so much more to do. Would that they were this far and it was only November. That's why I'm looking forward to trying the whole approach out in the fall, even if for some reason you can't formally set up a project.

Comments by V. W.

I'm a believer. What more can I say? The only thing I think you should do more about is a project for principals and teachers reluctant to adopt the program. The fact that we reinforce each other negatively and positively in life all the time should be stressed. Behavior modification is not manipulation or bribery — this should be stressed.

A hundred thanks to everyone for assistance and support. I really don't know if I would have been able to finish this school year without [the consultant's] support, encouragement, and skill at getting across all points of the program. I felt we worked well together. Your staff seems well organized, concerned, and knowledgeable.

I must say a few things about behavior modification and traditional classroom management. Sometimes it seems that a firm "stop that" or "get your hands off him" are necessary. The children in this neighborhood respect these kinds of statements. They even comment on the fact that I am handling the situations. If a child tells me his pencil is missing, his face looks relieved when I state loudly and firmly that "pencils are to be left alone," "keep your hands off other people's pencils," or "Michael's mother doesn't buy his pencils for other kids to take." The pencil may not be found, but Michael feels as though I took care of the situation.

Sometimes I run out of patience and, for my own release, I yell or send a kid home if he doesn't work. *This* helps me out on those days when the pressure rises.

I feel that the two biggest changes I have made this year are the following:

1. I don't spend my emotional energy on kids who act up. I have made a turnabout and pay attention to those who follow rules and work. I find I feel better about coming to work in the morning, and I don't feel defeated when I go home at night thinking about the kids who don't control themselves and don't work. I keep the memories with me of those who really benefit from a teacher who works hard.
2. I feel as though the five rules and fine charts have helped me make clear my standards. Before, I always had classes with a great amount of internal control. This year I didn't. So my quasi-open class teaching methods didn't work. I *had* to tighten up. In the future I think I will start off tight, somewhat rigid, and then loosen up. For example, I'll begin by handing out and locking up art supplies and gradually begin leaving some out for general use. I'll take the boys to the bathroom and tell them to "use it" one-by-one and come out and line up again. I'll do this at

first and then lighten up later.

All that's left to say is many, many thanks for everything!

Comments by E. T.

Room 205 is a classroom of thirty children between the ages of eight and twelve who are labeled low achievers and slow learners. The reading levels of the children range from pre-primer to second grade. There are thirty students who are failing to learn, have no motivation, and don't care. These children are in school because they have to be. Their parents, for the most part, are apathetic.

Michael didn't care, he didn't try. He never finished his work on time because his mind wandered. Although Michael's mother was one of the few parents who showed an interest in her child, she was slowly giving up. She had gone from talking to him, to taking things away, to physical punishment — with no results.

Gwendolyn needed all the attention. She got her attention because she was so disruptive. During a lesson, shouting or turning and slugging another child was common. Other children followed her example because she was so successful. Talking to her mother produced no results.

Carl had just given up — he knew he couldn't do anything. He lacked all motivation. When he was cajoled into doing his work, he reacted violently. He was one of nine children of a parent who didn't have time to talk to teachers.

As their teacher I was faced with the major problem of disciplining the children to do some work and motivating them enough to really want to try. By halfway through the year I was somewhat successful with some of the children. Candy rewards for doing good work reached some of them. Negative reinforcement with punishment and yelling reached some others, but there was a core group of about eight children that nothing I could think of helped.

Then behavior modification came to our school and to my classroom. This program hinged completely on me. If I changed my behavior, there was a direct impact on the children. I turned from using negative reinforcement to all positive reinforcement and ignoring behavior that wasn't acceptable. I reinforced only the child who was following the rules we set up at the beinning of the program. I had to be consistent in order for it to work. Anyone who wasn't following the rules just did not get reinforced or get any of my attention.

The crux of the program was a point system. Each child received a point for each rule followed in a given time period. The rules we drew up for my classroom were (1) staying in your seat, (2) working hard, (3) raising your hand for recognition, (4) ignoring someone bothering you, and (5) not disturbing others. The rules were acted out and discussed several times a week or when needed. A poster with the rules and pictures was put up to remind the children.

Every day each child was given a point sheet with these rules and boxes for earned points. At 10:30 AM, noon, 2:00 PM, and 3:00 PM each child received the points earned along with a little conversation about his or her progress. Here again I had to emphasize the improvement and all the good things they did — and ignore or barely touch upon poor behavior.

Two bonus points a day were given for exceptional behavior; this took into consideration the individual's improvement and capabilities. I gave these points for finishing work on time, not hitting another child back, starting work on time, turning in a lost pencil or dime, reading a book, or doing extra work. A child lost a point for each rule he didn't follow. If a child reacted to the point of hurting another child or was disrupting too many children, he was warned. If he still continued the behavior, he was fined 2 points. If he still continued, he had to leave the classroom for fifteen minutes to go to an isolated area for time-out.

I had a score sheet with me at all times containing each child's name, codes for the rules, and the time allotment boxes. This enabled me to keep track of each child's behavior and score throughout the day.

At the end of the day every child received a prize for earning 16 out of the possible 22 points. The responsibility for following the rules was on the children. They themselves had "messed up" if they didn't get a prize.

During this part of the first phase of the program, about four weeks, I saw a drastic reduction in negative behavior. Just to earn their points and their prizes the children began to work harder and not act up so much. As every day went by I gradually increased my expectations for each child. The problem would be to keep this enthusiasm going as I gradually phased out the tangible rewards by replacing them with my praise and grades.

In phase 2 of the program things got harder for the children. I still made my "rounds" to talk to each child four times a day, but now they received the points they earned at noon and 3 PM. They now needed to earn 17 points to get their prize, a grade of E. After earning three E's the child received a prize (larger than the one in phase 1). My expectations were still increasing and the children were still improving. They were staying quieter for longer periods of time and getting more work done. They were even improving academically because now their efforts were aimed at earning points instead of disrupting the classroom.

In phase 3, each child needed to earn six E's to get his or her final big prize. From there they went on to earn E's for their report card: Two more E's for an E in Courtesy, three for an E in Conduct, four for an E in Social Habits, and five for an E in Work Habits. The tangible rewards were gone. Every child worked for my praise, my attention, and grades. Before they never cared about grades, but now this is what they wanted and worked for. The chart we had up with their names and all the E's they had earned became one of the most important things in the room. If they missed an E one day, they really felt bad and worked harder the next day. The fear I had at the beginning of the program that the children would not respond to grades instead of tangible rewards did not materialize. The program was a success.

I began to feel that I was really teaching. In these two months I could see tremendous improvement! The improvement in behavior led directly to academic improvement in all subjects. I could conduct three reading groups, a spelling lesson, and a phonics lesson each morning with few interruptions. A science discussion with almost every child involved could last twenty minutes. And what learning! The kids discovered they could really think.

Their opinions of themselves really improved, and the classroom took on a happier atmosphere. They no longer felt stigmatized for being in the "dummy" class. They were learning harder math than most of the other fourth grades, and they knew it. They felt great. If things began to fall apart, a review of the point makers (rules) and a five-minute pep talk brought everything together again.

Michael is still low academically and his mind wanders from time to time, but now he finishes his work on time and sometimes goes on to earn extra credit. He is trying, and I can see some academic improvement.

Gwendolyn still needs that attention, but now she works hard to get positive reinforcement. She smiles more, as do all the kids. Gwen has taken it upon herself to help straighten out the kids that start messing up. "You're gonna lose that point!" she'd say. Every now and then she shouts out, but this is ignored and soon she's back to work again.

Since the program started, Carl has not reacted violently. He is one of the hardest workers in the class, and now he gets disturbed if someone acts up in class. He does everything he can to please me and get recognition. Carl now thinks he's just as good as anyone else.

This, I feel, is one of the strongest points of the behavior modification program. The children have a positive image of themselves and a more positive attitude towards school. They now have more motivation to learn and to try. They have felt success. They don't give up; they found they can do it!

The time I spent yelling at and threatening the children and frustrating myself and them is now used for teaching and talking positively with the children. There is a better overall atmosphere and better relationships among the children and between the children and me.

I'm convinced this program can work and work well. I feel success, and the children feel success. We're happy. Next year I will use the ideas I learned and implement my own program, but on a smaller scale.

Comments by J. K.

I have tried to comment on the suggested topics, but I would rather write about the results of the program.

THE CLASSROOM IN GENERAL: The children in my class are academically slow and, I would say, hyperactive with short attention spans. They were grouped together in kindergarten because they were slow, non-English-speaking, or had behavior problems. In first grade they all spoke at least a little English, but six or seven children who had been retained were also added to the class.

At the beginning of the program the classroom was not only disruptive but positively destructive. Unless I spent every moment with the children, unpredictable things happened. This situation made it next to impossible to teach reading groups or to do any other kind of group work. The noise level was always very high.

Because definite rules were set up and I had a measure to be consistent with, everyone better understood what was expected of him or her. Rewards and punishments were consistent and predictable and were given as unemotionally as possible.

The class settled down considerably. The noise level became more bearable, although outsiders might find that hard to believe. Objects are no longer thrown through the air. No one has been stabbed with a pencil or scissors. Fights have diminished; even squabbles have lessened. The teacher may actually maintain her sanity — what's left of it anyway.

INDIVIDUAL STUDENTS: First let me say that not everyone has changed from a demon to an angel. But several children have changed drastically and I'd like to tell you about a few of them.

After the program had been in effect for about a week (during which time I thought I'd lose my mind), I suddenly realized that a little girl, Jennifer, who had formerly been a real pest (always at my desk, always running up to me), had not come up to my desk without permission for two days! That was a turning point in my belief that all this could really work.

Teresa was a constant fighter and tattletale who got little work done. She now works very hard and because she must raise her hand before speaking she tattles less frequently.

Michael, with encouragement and interest from home, has channeled his spare-time interests. He will read a book instead of throwing a crayon or color instead of throwing a milk carton. He had trouble at first because he is bright and self-directed, but he kept "self-directing" himself out of his chair to more interesting places, like the window or garbage can.

Steven was a major problem. He was a real terror, starting vicious fights without provocation, refusing to work, throwing tantrums, and not responding to reinforcers. Lately he has become more manageable. After exhausting every possiblity, I simply decided that I didn't care about him, didn't try to get him to earn points, etc. If he were good and I noticed, I would respond. And he is changing. (Something good must also be happening at home.) He is still disruptive but now it is his loud mouth rather than fights.

These are just a few of the children. The changes have been endless — everything from walking into the room and going straight to their seats to having about ten whole minutes in a day when I can sit down without monitoring the room.

CHANGES IN TEACHER BEHAVIOR: Since this was my first year of teaching, I think the program has had a great effect upon me. It is very easy to become a frustrated, screaming old grouch. I didn't go into teaching to become an animal trainer, to demean children or physically abuse them. But when such techniques are the models around you and your situation becomes more frustrating each day, such attitudes are slowly picked up.

This program forced me to look for good behavior. Finding that children are being good is rewarding and uplifting to me, and telling them so brings pleasure to all of us. Since I see good things, I am more alert to their appearance.

I think a great deal of maturing has happened too. I don't get frustrated to the point of being in knots. I don't want to strike out at some child who has cruelly wronged another child. I feel more calm and self-assured, in control of what is happening and more able to control myself.

AMOUNT OF TIME AND EFFORT REQUIRED IN RELATION TO RESULTS: The amount of time is endless and the effort is endless. The results are worth every minute.

Teaching takes time and effort, so why not channel your energy. It takes as much and probably more energy to become furious and charge across the room at some six-year-old as it does to circle the room writing down points and complimenting thirty-two children.

I would have gone to any extreme to gain some control over these children. Any time spent preparing for it was worth it. And the time taken out of their day was worth it, too, because they were already wasting time nonconstructively and this program gave me the control to teach the material they needed to know. If a child can't sit down, be quiet, and listen, then he is never going to learn to read. Behavior that is acceptable to schools as we know them is basic and precedes any kind of academics.

CLASSROOM PROGRAM DEFICITS: None that I can think of. There were a few handicaps. A very important one was that there was no available time-out place for disruptive students. Another was that such a program hadn't been tried before with such young children in as large a group. This was a problem because we all had to feel our way through situations — such as how long to maintain daily reinforcers, how often the children should be rated on their point slips, whether they need point slips after a certain period, whether notes to parents are reinforcers, and whether they understand grades and associate an E+ with higher achievement than an E-.

PROGRAM STRONG POINTS: There are so many that it's hard to know where to begin.

Such a program cannot go unnoticed, so you have to try to explain it to other teachers. Some of them pick up techniques like noticing good children and *telling them* that this behavior is noticed. We too frequently see good behavior but only make examples of poor behavior.

Having observers is a tremendous advantage. Because they are watching and not actively involved, they can see things you miss, make you aware of situations, like someone sitting quietly, and cue you if you fail to respond. They find simple solutions to problems that seem baffling simply because the teacher is too involved. An example of problems I had involved lining up and the end of the day procedure; I worked and struggled with these problems with no success. A few suggestions from the consultant about placing events in logical order and the end of the day went much smoother. I was amazed that it was all so easy and wondered why I hadn't thought of such a simple solution.

Most important, observers give the teacher constructive ideas and the positive reinforcement so desperately needed during the difficult phases of the program. Everyone needs a pat on the back, and many times there is little else immediately reinforcing the teacher.

On the lighter side, I have the only first-grade class that not only recognizes the word "aggression" but can define it as well!

MEETINGS OUTSIDE THE CLASSROOM: Absolutely essential — I don't see how else the program could work. I would be surprised that anyone who refused to meet outside class time would be willing to try this program.

I think meetings should be held at least once a week — more often to begin with. Topics should include theory if the teachers need it. I found it necessary to have some things clarified that related directly to my teaching. This information was usually presented informally. Classroom set-up and program changes should also be discussed. Most often, however, specific problems and situations need to be discussed. I thought the end of the week was a good time for these meetings because it made it possible for the teacher to introduce program changes early in the next week. It helps the children if their schedules are not changed in the middle of the week.

OVERALL STRENGTHS AND DEFICIENCIES: The people I worked with were fantastic. I could easily relate to them. They were patient and understanding and always one step ahead of whatever was happening. The program was very well organized.

The classroom rules, as set up, were far broader than I had ever thought about. As behavior and events changed, the rules were flexible enough to encompass most situations without stretching them too far. For example, aggression was first defined in the rules as hurting someone else or destroying someone else's property. It was modified to potentially hurting oneself, i.e. sliding down the railings. "Do not disturb others" meant that the students had to clean up the room because the janitor was disturbed by a messy room and it could be applied to disturbing another classroom as we walked through the halls. "Sitting at your desk facing forward" meant or came to mean that it must be your desk, it must be in its proper place (not switching seats), and you had to sit at it, not on top of or under it.

I can't think of any training deficiencies. Everyone worked with me a great deal and made sure I knew what I was doing before I had to do it. I was even given specially worked out procedures for how to present the program and program changes.

INTEREST IN FUTURE PARTICIPATION: I am most anxious to try this program in the fall, especially since I'll be better prepared. Also, I'd like to start it with the children fresh. I'd like to start off with only one set of rules and one schedule of events. I had tried so many approaches by March when the program began that I think it lost some of its effectiveness.

I am anxious to try the program with more things under control. March was too late to start such a program, and I think that as well as things have turned out, they could have been better had everything started earlier. So I am very much looking forward to the fall and to seeing what results can be obtained under optimum conditions.

ADDITIONAL COMMENTS: Many thanks for allowing me to participate in this program and especial thanks to [the consultants] for all your help and unending patience.

Thanks again.

Comments by B. L.

I first came in contact with the [school consultants] at an in-service meeting for first-year teachers. I felt a great need for an organized program like this in order to gain control within my class. Fortunately, I was given the opportunity to participate. The results of my participation were very positive classroom changes.

The first step in the program was identifying problem areas. My class, in part, consisted of five EMH students who were constantly aggressive towards each other and myself. Little teaching or learning could take place; most of my time was spent attending to the problems and disturbances of these children. The next step was to set up a way to deal with the behaviors of these students.

The most important part of the whole program was finding a constructive and consistent way of interacting with the students. With the help of [the consultants], I was able to devise a successful method for dealing with disruptive behavior. By ignoring the disruptions and attending to those students on task, disruptions became fewer and fewer. Constant verbal praise for good behavior was needed and used throughout the program.

Though verbal praise was the most important reinforcer, additional tangible reinforcers were needed in my class. In the first two months of the program, toys and candy were given at the end of the day to those students earning a given number of points; however, this method of reinforcement proved unsuccessful in my class. Since the attention span of the students was very short, waiting to the end of the day for their reward was too long. The students earned points on their point slip at specific spaced intervals. If they did not follow a given rule during a certain span of time, a zero was put on their point slip. Often when a zero was placed on a student's point slip, the student would become very disruptive and destructive. A change in the program was needed at this point. The reinforcement of toys and candy at the end of the day was removed. Instead, the students were able to earn candy at random times throughout the day. The individual point slips were removed. I kept a record on a master chart of all the points earned during the day. A child could earn points any time he was following a specific rule. Since there were no more zeros, the students did not become as frustrated. Also, the students who were on task were rewarded immediately through either a point on my master chart or some consummable tangible.

Other successful reinforcers used in my room were daily E's and an E chart, parent good notes, and activity periods. If a student exhibited good behavior through most of the day, he earned an E on his E chart and a note to take home to his parents stating the present number of E's earned. The notes helped my students recognize their good behavior and made them proud of themselves.

The change in my class was not a sudden one, it was gradual. The students began to work a lot harder and fight a lot less. Before the program, there were frequent emotional outbursts such as a student throwing objects or running in and out of the room. This rarely occurred after the program was in full operation.

I also discovered a change in myself as the program progressed. As the students began to respond more to my lessons, I began to feel much more confident of my teaching ability. By observing and discussing the videotapes of my classroom, I was better able to recognize my weaknesses. The team that initiated the program in my room was very efficient and helpful.

Best of all, the [consultation] provided me with a variety of successful teaching strategies for use in future years.

Comments by M. R.

In late December I was asked by my principal about my willingness to participate in the [teacher consultation program]. Although I was barely acquainted with behavior modification, I was willing to try anything at this point because of the problems I was encountering in my classroom. (This was only my second year of teaching and I had nothing to replace the idealistic "love the children and everything else will work out" philosophy that I had left college with.) The children I work with had no inner discipline to call on in nonstructured situations. Whenever I tried to open things up, chaos developed. After the first few weeks of school, tighter and tighter discipline became necessary to keep them in line. Disruptions were common and couldn't be ignored as they usually resulted in fights. Good students received little attention from me because I spent a good part of the day attending to the disruptive ones. And the number of disruptive students grew larger since their behavior was being attended to.

The program set up for me began in January and produced immediate results. Elements of the program included establishing five basic rules — listed on two charts posted in the classroom — posting an additional sign for bonus points and a list of causes for being fined, individual point slips to be pasted on each child's desk each day, candy and small toys used as reinforcers, and me. Later in the program, when the tangible reinforcers were dropped and children began earning E's, an E chart with everyone's name on it, superstar name tags, and good notes to parents were added to the program. Emphasis was placed on reviewing the rules every morning, reminders that everyone who followed the rules would win a prize, a display of the prizes, and student role-playing of the rules. I had four specific times during the day to circulate around the room, record points, and talk to each student about his work and conduct. Mainly, the positive aspects of each student's work and conduct were discussed, with the negative aspects introduced almost as an afterthought. This routine, circulating around the room, is still going on although points have been dropped for three of these times. In between these times I cued students by calling attention to those who were following the rules. Eventually, it was enough for the students to see me with my clipboard (teacher's chart of student points) walking around; this became an instant reminder of the rules they should be following.

The immediate result has been a classroom with minimal noise and a lot more work in the mornings (we have seatwork and reading groups all morning) and a much more attentive group in the afternoon when we have group work, class discussions, and activity periods. By the third week of the program, the number of students completing their daily assignments went from three or four to fifteen or seventeen. Needless to say, grades began to rise and delight in achievement began to show on the faces of many students I thought would never progress.

Several months after the program began, I found things getting noisy and work dropping off again. With the help of the [consultants and their videotapes and discussions] I realized it was caused by me. Instead of continuing with constant positive reinforcement and cueing, I was getting angry at the students when they weren't following the rules; I had reasoned that by now they knew how and were capable of behaving correctly and working on their own. True reasoning but faulty tactics! The day after viewing my "old angry self" on tape, I began an all-out-effort to go back to the cueing and reinforcing of good behavior, and the program worked again, instantly. My classroom was back on track that day.

I found nothing lacking in the services. The outlines [the consultants] supplied me with and the discussions with them gave me a basic understanding of behavior modification techniques. The texts, however, I found practically useless. Without the meetings and evaluations, I'm sure the program would not have worked. My only complaint is that I received so much positive reinforcement that I felt behavior modification was being used on me.

I am confident that the skills I gained will carry me through the rest of my teaching career. Next September I plan to begin the year using some type of E chart and weekly good notes to parents, but my emphasis will be on my positive interactions with the students. It is delightful for me to be able to say so many good things to my students; this technique helps teachers and pupils become happier people.

As a final note, I found the visits from [the consultant] especially important to me during the transition period. They served as constant reminders to me not to slip back into the old way of doing things. It is so easy to get involved with desk work and such when the room is quiet, but only by consistency in teacher interactions with students will the good results continue. I will always be grateful to the people who helped me so much and thankful that I was able to participate in this program.

Appendix I
GLOSSARY

Activity reinforcers: Enjoyable events involving the motor behaviors of an individual, events that are used as reinforcers (sports, field trips, etc.).

Antecedent: A stimulus element or event in an individual's environment that immediately precedes a response by that individual.

Aversive stimulus: An unpleasant and undesired stimulus whose termination increases the frequency of a response or whose presentation decreases the frequency of a response that it follows.

Avoidance behavior: Behavior that results in the postponement of an aversive stimulus.

Baseline: A preintervention record of behavior, recorded in terms of frequency, duration, or intensity, and establishing a reference from which the effects of subsequent intervention are assessed.

Behavior: Any activity by an individual that can be observed and measured.

Coding: The use of symbols to represent behaviors to be recorded during observation periods.

Consequence: An element of an individual's environment that follows a response.

Contingency contract: An agreement between two or more people that specifies a criterion for a desired behavior to be performed by one and the reinforcer to be delivered by the other when the criterion is fulfilled.

Continuous Reinforcement: A schedule of reinforcement during which every occurrence of a specified response is reinforced.

Cue: A stimulus that sets the occasion for the occurrence of a particular response.

Deprivation: The withholding of a reinforcer for a period of time in order to increase its reinforcing value.

Discrimination: The occurrence or nonoccurrence of a particular response controlled by the presence or absence of particular environmental stimuli.

Duration: A period of time during which a behavior continues.

Environment: All the stimuli surrounding an individual, including people, places, events, and norms.

Escape behavior: A response that terminates an aversive stimulus.

Extinction: A decline in the rate of occurrence of a response resulting from the termination of reinforcement.

Fading: A procedure for gradually changing the control of an individual's performance from one stimulus to another.

Frequency: The number of times a specified response occurs within a given amount of time.

Generalization: The process whereby a response learned in one stimulus situation is transferred to other similar situations.

Incompatible behavior: A behavior, the occurrence of which, precludes the occurrence of another, usually undesirable, behavior.

Intensity: The degree of strength or force with which a response is made.

Intermittent reinforcement: A schedule of reinforcement during which the performance of a specified behavior is periodically — not continuously — reinforced.

Labeling: To describe a person or set of behaviors in terms of general categories that are not descriptive of specific observable behaviors.

Modeling: The performance or demonstration of a behavior by one person followed by the imitation of that behavior by another.

Monitoring: Recording the incidence of a behavior.

Negative reinforcement: The removal of an aversive stimulus immediately following and contingent upon a response, increasing the probability of future occurrences of that response.

Negative reinforcer: An aversive stimulus that is to be terminated after the occurrence of a response, thus increasing that response.

Neutral stimulus: A stimulus with no eliciting, reinforcing, or punishing, properties.

Points: A mark on a slip of paper whose value depends on the ability to exchange it for primary reinforcers.

Positive reinforcement: The presentation of a stimulus immediately following and contingent upon a response, a stimulus increasing the probability of the future occurrence of that response.

Positive reinforcer: A stimulus that is to be presented after the occurrence of a response, thus increasing that response.

Punishment: A procedure in which a response is followed by either the presentation of an aversive stimulus or the removal of a positive reinforcer, either action resulting in a reduction of the response they follow.

Rehearsal: The practice of skills in a simulated setting that is representative of the setting in which the skills are to be used.

Reinforcement: The presentation of a positive or negative reinforcer resulting in an increase in the probability of the future occurrence of the response it follows.

Reinforcer: An element or event in an individual's environment increasing the frequency of the response it follows.

Response: Any form of behavior used as a unit of measurement or description.

Role-playing: A training technique in which an individual assumes and behaves in a manner appropriate to a given role.

Satiation: The decrease in the effectiveness of a reinforcer resulting from excessive repeated presentation.
Shaping: The reinforcement of successive improvements an individual makes in learning a behavior.
Situation: The total of all internal and external stimuli that act upon an individual in a given setting at a given time.
Social reinforcer: A reinforcer that is produced through the interaction of two or more people.
Stimulus: Elements of an individual's environment that influence that individual's behavior.
Superstitious behavior: A behavior that occurs because of an accidental, temporal relationship between that behavior and another event, a relationship erroneously interpreted as a cause and effect.
Tangible reinforcer: Material objects used as positive reinforcers.
Target behavior: The specified behavior to be changed.
Time-out: A procedure in which, as a result of engaging in undesirable behaviors, an individual is removed from a reinforcing situation and placed in a neutral setting.

Appendix 2

SELECTED READINGS

The following books and articles are provided for or suggested to the participating teachers:

Carter, R. D. *Help! These kids are driving me crazy.* Champaign: Research Press, 1972.

Kuypers, D. S., Becker, W. C., and O'Leary, K. D. How to make a token system fail. *Except Chil, 35:*101-109, 1968.

Madsen, C. H. and Madsen, C. K. *Teaching discipline.* Boston: Allyn and Bacon, 1974.

O'Leary, K. D. and O'Leary, S. G. *Classroom management: The successful use of behavior modification.* Elmsford: Pergamon Press, 1972.

Poulos, R. W. and Devine, V. T. Tangible reinforcers: Bonuses or bribes? *J Consul Clin Psych, 38:*1-8, 1972.

Thomas, D. R., Becker, W. C., and Armstrong, M. Production and elimination of disruptive classroom behavior by systematically varying teacher's behavior. *J Applied Beh Analy, 1*:35-45, 1968.

INDEX

A "Forms and samples" entry is included in this index. This entry lists the forms, sample letters, summaries, outlines, and checklists that a consultant may use or provide to teachers during consultations.

A

Agenda for consultation
  assessing problem student behaviors, 52-54
  developing positive teacher-student interactions, 93-94
  identifying positive reinforcers, 76-77
  measuring behaviors, 59-60
  specifying contingent relationships, 86-87
  specifying desirable student behaviors, 69-70
  specifying problem student behaviors, 42-44
Antecedents (*see* Cues and Problem student behaviors, precipitating conditions of)
Appropriate behavior (*see* Desirable student behaviors)
Assessment (*see also* Measuring behaviors and Observations)
  agenda for, 53-54
  assessment inventory form, 55
  cues and consequences, 50-51
  example of, 51
  precipitating conditions, 49
  problem student behaviors, 49-55
  teacher behaviors, 51-52
Avoidance, 28-29, 32, 36, 75
Awards (*see also* Reinforcers)
  presentation of, 126-127

B

Behavior (*see also* Desirable student behaviors and Problem student behaviors)
  changing of, 30-33
  deficits in, 41-42, 65
  definition of, 25-26
  excesses in, 41
  learning of, 27-30
  long and short term goals, 67-68
  vs. emotions and feelings, 25, 35
  vs. inferences, 25-27
  vs. symptoms, 35
Behavioral principles, 24-36
  behaviors as learned, 27-30
  changing of behaviors, 30-33
  problems as behaviors, 24-27
  table of, 29
  teacher as a change agent, 33-34
  teacher concerns about (*see* Concerns of teachers, about behavioral principles)
Bribery, 35

C

Class schedule
  example form, 46
Classroom management program, 95-137
Classroom rules, 69, 98-99
  poster of, 98
Concerns of teachers (*see also* Teacher evaluations and comments)
  about behavioral principles, 34-36
  during negotiations, 17-20
  initial meetings, 145-151
Conditioned reinforcers (*see* Reinforcers, social)
Consequences, 28-30, 41, 50-51 (*see also* Reinforcement and Punishment)

Consultant
  log of, 141-170
  responsibilities of, 7-9, 16 (*see also* Negotiations, sample of agreements)
  restrictions on, 5
  role of, 5-13
  teacher concerns about, 18
Consultation (*see also* Negotiations)
  agendas for (*see* Agendas for consultation)
  preparation for, 3
  resources for, 16-17
  sample letter to school, 10
  sample proposal, 11-13
  targets of, 6
  tasks and goals of, 6-7
  teacher evaluations of, outline, 171
  vs. therapy, 7-8
  writing the proposal, 141-142
Contingencies, 32-33, 79-87
  agenda for specifying, 86-87
  consistency in, 32, 83
  definition of, 32, 79
  explicit and implicit, 85-86
  feedback for, 81-82
  if-then, 79-80
  individual and group, 83-85
  mutually acceptable, 80-81
Contracts
  contingency, 83-84
Cues, 27-28, 32-34, 50-51

D

Data (*see* Observations)
Deprivation
  access to reinforcers, 74
Desirable student behaviors, 65-70
  agenda for specifying, 70
  behavioral deficits, 65-66
  classroom rules, 69-70
  examples of, 66
  incompatable behaviors, 66-67
  long and short term goals, 67-68
  teacher concerns about, 155-159
Disruptive behaviors (*see* Problem student behaviors)
Duration, 57

E

Environmental stimuli (*see* Stimuli)
Escape, 28-29, 32, 36, 75
Ethical issues (*see* Concerns of teachers, about behavioral principles)
Evaluation of teachers (*see* Teacher, evaluation of)
Extinction, 28, 29

F

Feedback
  components of, 81-82
Forms and samples
  assessment inventory form, 55
  certificate of merit, 135
  class schedule form, 46
  classroom rules poster, 98
  consent to videotape, 23
  consultation proposal, 11-13
  daily checklist, 124-125
  E chart, 101
  good note, 132
  graph of changes in behavior, 63
  letter of teacher recognition, 136-137
  letter to a school, 10
  letter to parents, 23
  list of reinforcers, 78
  negotiation agreements, 21-22
  observation format and form, 61-62
  observation notes form, 48
  point slip, 119
  preparation before program, checklist, 121
  procedures for award presentation, 126-127
  seating chart, 47
  student information form, 45
  summaries of phases in classroom management program, 128-134
  teacher interaction record, 64
  teacher outline for introducing program, 122-123
  teacher record, 120
  teacher-student interaction guidelines, 110-112
  time-out slip, 78

Index

Frequency, 57

G

Generalization
  desirable behaviors, 50
  stimulus, 29-30
Goals of consultation (*see* Consultation, tasks and goals of)

H

Hyperactivity
  example of, 26

I

Ignoring (*see* Teacher-student interaction, disruptive behavior)
Implementation of point system (*see* Point system)
Inappropriate behaviors (*see* Problem student behaviors)
Incompatible behaviors, 30-31, 66-67
Inferences (*see* Behavior, vs. inferences)
In-service presentation
  experiences with, 144-145
Intensity, 57
Interactions (*see* Teacher-student interaction)
Labeling, 39-40
Log, consultant's (*see* Consultant, log of)
Low-frequency behaviors
  increasing, 31

M

Measuring behaviors, 56-64 (*see also* Observations)
  agenda for, 59-60
  baseline and treatment, 58
  purpose of, 56
  recording behaviors, 57
  teacher behaviors, 58-59
Modeling, 31, 81
  teacher practice, 159-163

N

Negotiations, 14-23
  conditions of consultation, 15-17
  experience with principals, 142-144
  experience with teachers, 145-146
  limitations on the consultation, 17
  purpose of consultation, 15
  sample of agreements, 21-22
  teacher concerns about, 17-19
Neutral stimuli, 28

O

Observations
  baseline and treatment, 58
  classroom, 96-97
  codes for, 57, 113
  experiences during, 151-153
  format and form for, 61-62
  graph, 63
  observation notes form, 48
  recording student behaviors, 57
  teacher behaviors, 58-59
  teacher interaction record, 64
  usefulness of, 40
Off-task behaviors (*see* Problem student behaviors)
On-task behaviors (*see* Desirable student behaviors)

P

Parents
  consent of, 16
  letter to, 23
Peer influence, 85
Phases of point system (*see* Point system, phases in and summary of phases)
Point slip
  example of, 119
  instructions for, 113-119
Point system
  award presentation, 126-127
  bonus points, 105-106
  certificate of merit, 135
  daily checklist, 124-125
  E chart, 101

experiences with implementing, 164-169
fines, 106-107
functions of, 107
good note, 132
introducing to class, 122-123
phases in, 99-105
point periods, 97 (*see also* Specific phases)
preparation for, 121
recording points (*see* Point slip, instructions for)
summary of phase 1, 128-129
summary of phase 2, 130
summary of phase 3, 131
summary of phase 4, 133
summary of phase 5, 134
table of phases, 105
teacher concerns about, 167-169
teacher record, 120
Praise (*see* Reinforcers, social)
Predispositions (*see* Teacher, predispositions of)
Principal
  responsibilities of, 16 (*see also* Negotiations, sample of agreements)
Principles of behavior (*see* Behavioral principles)
Problem solving
  steps of, 37
Problem student behaviors, 24-27, 39-48
  agenda for specifying, 42-44
  assessment of (*see* Assessment, problem student behaviors)
  definition of, 39
  examples of, v-vi, 25, 30, 51
  experiences in specifying, 153-155
  precipitating conditions of, 49
  severity of, 57
  teacher comments about, 171-189
  teacher expectations, 25
Punishment, 28-29, 32, 36, 75-76 (*see also* Time-out)

R

Reinforcement, 28-29 (*see also* Awards, presentation of and Reinforcers)
  immediacy of, 74
Reinforcers, 71-78

activities, 72
agenda for identifying, 76-77
definition of, 71
effectiveness of, 74-75
examples of, 78
intent vs. effect, 71-72
natural, 36, 104
selection of, 74
social, 72, 82
tangible, 36, 73-74, 82
teacher (*see* Teacher, reinforcers for)
types of, 72-73
Reprimands, 89, 90, 91 (*see also* Teacher-student interaction, disruptive behaviors)
Role-playing, 81 (*see also* Modeling)
Rules (*see* Classroom rules)

S

Satiation
  access to reinforcers, 74
Seating chart
  example form, 47
Self-management, 95, 103, 104
Shaping, 31, 68-69, 81
Stimuli, 27-28, 51
Student information
  example form, 45

T

Target behaviors
  student (*see* Classroom rules)
  teacher (*see* Consultation, tasks and goals of)
Teacher
  assessment of, 51-52
  comments (*see* Teacher evaluations and comments)
  concerns (*see* Concerns of teachers)
  cooperation of, 17-18
  evaluation of, 16
  experiences with, 145-148
  interaction with students (*see* Teacher-student interaction)
  letter of recognition for, 136-137
  observations of (*see* Observations, teacher behaviors)

predispositions of, 40
problem behaviors of, 92-93
record (*see* Teacher record)
reinforcers for, 8-9
reluctance of, 15-16
responsibilities of, 16, 33-34, 49-50 (*see also* Negotiations, sample of agreements)
self-recording, 58-59
voluntary participation of, 15-16
Teacher evaluations and comments, 171-189
Teacher record
 example of, 120
 instructions for, 113-119
Teacher-student interaction, 88-94, 107-112 (*see also* Feedback)
 agenda for developing, 93-94
 disruptive behaviors, 106-107, 112
 exceptionally good behaviors, 105-106
 guidelines for, 88-92, 110-112
 types of situations, 112
Therapy vs. consultation (*see* Consultation, vs. therapy)
Time-out, 76, 78, 106-107
 example form, 78

V

Verbalizations
 as behaviors, 27
Videotape consent, 16
 example form, 23
Voluntary participation of teachers (*see* Teacher, voluntary participation of)